The Story of the
Quilt of Hope

Threads of Unlived Lives: Clerical Child Sexual Abuse

Copyright © 2022 Adrianne Moloney

Adrianne Moloney has asserted her right under the Copyright, Designs and Patents Act 1988 to be identified as the author of this work. The information in this book is based on the author's experiences and opinions. The publisher specifically disclaims responsibility for any adverse consequences, which may result from use of the information contained herein.

All rights reserved. No part of this publication may be reproduced, stored in or introduced into a retrieval system, or transmitted in any form, or by any means (electronic, mechanical, photocopying, recording or otherwise) without the prior written permission of the author. Any person who does any unauthorised acts in relation to this publication will be liable to criminal prosecution and civil claims for damages. Enquiries should be made through the publisher.

First published by Turtle Publishing 2022

Cover design by Turtle Publishing
Layout and typesetting by Turtle Publishing

ISBN: 978-0-6453954-6-4 (paperback)
ISBN: 978-0-6453954-7-1 (ebook)

turtlepublishing.com.au

We dedicate this book to all
those impacted by clerical child
sexual abuse.

May your voice be heard.

Silence, they say, is the voice
of complicity.
But silence is impossible.
Silence screams.
Silence is the message, just as
doing nothing is an act.

Leonard Peltier

Table of Contents

Foreword	ix
A note from the author	xiii
Acknowledgements	xv

PART A
Power, Secrecy and Betrayal

1	Clerical Power and Pastoral Care. How did it come to this?	5
2	Moving Towards Justice	17
3	The Quilt of Hope	41

PART B
Stories of Hope and Despair

4	The Burden of Unbearable Knowledge	53
5	The Ripple Effects	69
6	A Mother's Fight for Justice	89
7	Memoirs of a Catholic School Teacher	107
8	Lives Lost	131
9	Patchwork of Lives	143

Recommended Reading	156
Postscript	157
Appendix A	159
Appendix B	167

FOREWORD

The Hope in the Quilt
Lawrence Moloney

Hope is at the core of our continuity
You could say it's in our DNA
Hope sustains our present
And feeds our future imaginings
Hope is a reservoir to call on
When events threaten our stability
Through hope we regain our balance
We recalibrate our moral compass

Hope is the birthright of our children
Through the loving care of others
Their fears are acknowledged and assuaged
Their curiosities are encouraged and tempered
The hope in our children's eyes
Grows through a thousand loving encounters
Hope gives children confidence
That wounds can always be healed
And safe places can always be found

Christians place hope in a loving God
An archetypal loving parent
His command was simple and profound
Love each other as I love you
Of those who preach in his name
Too many have betrayed the message
Too many have confused aspirations
With the trappings of ecclesiastical power
While those they feigned to serve
Became objects of personal ambitions
Ignored exploited even despised

It's a short step
From object to abuse
It's a short step
From sexual abuse
To the perverse logic
That this gross betrayal of trust
Is somehow linked to love
That this gross betrayal of trust
Is a private arrangement
With no links to privilege
With no links to power

We know now
How countless children suffered
From a shame that was not their shame
From an unforgivable conspiracy
Of silence and denial
We know now
How hope was ripped from their bodies
How hope died in their eyes
How they were suffocated
By the sham righteousness
Of a powerful and crumbling institution
Incapable of the very compassion
It required of others

Too many did not survive
Too many of the lives that continued
Were ruled by guilt and fearful confusion
Those who loved them
Shared their journey of helpless rage
Before a growing grasp
Of the magnitude of the betrayal
Gave rage its healing direction
Slowly but surely
Hope was rekindled
Through dogged persistence and bravery
Hope dared confront false power and false glory

This book is about The Quilt of Hope
Destined for proud and public display
Acknowledging a million tortured words
A million desperate tears
Reflecting the hopes of all mothers
Of all invested in the care of children
Crafted with love patience and defiance
It speaks for the many who have been silenced
Who will no longer be silenced
It speaks for itself.

A NOTE FROM THE AUTHOR

The Quilt of Hope was created in 2014 by a small group of parishioners in the Ballarat Diocese in response to revelations of clerical child sexual abuse in the Catholic church. It was a practical way to reach out to people at a time of active denial, deafening silence and concealment/cover-up from their spiritual leaders and wider congregation.

The Quilt of Hope serves as a memorial to the countless lives affected and provides the thread that connects a patchwork quilt of social history which otherwise may never have been told.

What started as a conversation between Carmel Moloney (aka my Mum) and me about developing a pamphlet to explain the Quilt of Hope transformed into the book you are now reading. We knew the Quilt of Hope and the voices behind the blocks that make up the quilt deserved and demanded more than a pamphlet.

Our original and quite ambitious intent was to identify the makers behind each of the blocks. Stories would be gathered over a cup of tea and the oral histories recorded to be later transcribed.

With the advent of the pandemic, border closures and lock downs became our new normal. This meant we were no longer able to hold gatherings that would provide the informal conversations and links to makers that we hoped for. Travelling to Victoria to meet with people and record their oral history became an impossibility.

Whilst the process and book structure changed throughout the journey, the intent of the book did not – to provide a vehicle for the voices behind the Quilt of Hope to be heard.

I cannot claim the title of author for this book. It has been a collaborative writing effort and I have been in the privileged position of facilitating the process and contributing some words where needed.

I am indebted to those who have contributed to the book and trusted me with their stories. Without their words the book would not have been possible. I am thankful to those who have given me their time to share their experiences and contribute to broadening my understanding of the issues.

The book is divided into two parts. The first part provides the background and social context in which the Quilt of Hope is located. This includes an account of how the group, 'Moving Towards Justice' was formed and their journey as parishioners grappling with the heinous acts of their church. The social and historical significance of textiles and quilts follows this and the making of the Quilt of Hope is described.

The second part presents the lived experiences of some parishioners, mothers, and truth seekers. Much of this has been written in their own words and provides a powerful insight into what they have lived through. These accounts reflect the many voices that need to be heard.

The impact of clerical child sexual abuse inflicted decades ago continues to be felt in the everyday lives of people. We hope the book contributes to the ongoing conversations needed to continue to break down the walls of silence and dispel the shame felt by so many.

> Hope is being able to see that there is light
> despite all of the darkness
>
> Bishop Desmond Tutu

ACKNOWLEDGEMENTS

The support I have received to complete the book has been immense. I am deeply grateful for the words of encouragement that reinforced to me how important the story is to so many.

Firstly, we want to thank all those who contributed to the making of the Quilt and particularly Beryl Andersen for her quilting expertise to bring the Quilt of Hope together.

To Diane, Helen, Ann, Kevin, Margaret, Mary, Stephanie, Gwen and Shirley for allowing us to use your words. The power of your stories speaks to us all. A special mention to Diane for sharing the writing journey with me – I will miss our catch ups to perfect a sentence or find the right word!

For supporting the process to get the book finalised I thank Mike Parer for the gentle nagging throughout the journey and sharing his publishing knowledge. To Alan Ryan for organising the Quilt to be photographed in Canberra and for the other images needed. To Lawrie Moloney for his guidance, sage words, constant reassurance, and patient editing of the book - I could not have done it without you. To Rach for the hours spent helping with organising files and some referencing. To Kathy from Turtle Publishing, thank you for appearing at a vital time and bringing the book to life in the way we had imagined.

To Mary Darcy for her wise words early in the journey and Anne O'Brien for helping where she could. To Heather O'Connor for looking at early drafts and being real with me as she has been throughout my life. To Mary and Carl Aiken for the editorial input during the critical final stages and providing me with words of reassurance. To my wonderful friends who are the best cheer squad anyone could have.

Thank you to everyone who contributed financially to the production and publishing of the book. We appreciate your generosity and support. A special mention to Paul Tatchell for supporting us in a multitude of ways.

To my beautiful daughter Beth who has endured the countless hours I have needed in front of the computer screen.

And finally, to my Mum - my guide, my mentor, my inspiration. Without her unconditional love and support I would not have been able to complete this important piece of work. It was for her that I wrote it, and I am extremely proud to call myself her daughter.

Quilt of Hope

PART A

Power, Secrecy and Betrayal

Chapter 1

Clerical Power and Pastoral Care. How did it come to this?

"I believe the root of all evil is abuse of power."
Patricia Cornwell

This book is set in the Diocese of Ballarat which is one of four Catholic dioceses within Victoria, Australia (the other 3 being Melbourne, Sale, and Sandhurst). The Diocese is divided into three zones northern, central, and southern and was established in 1874. It is the largest Diocese within the state, covering an area of 58,000km2 across the western half of the state from the Murray River to the Southern Ocean. As of March 2020, it is reported as having 41 parishes comprising one hundred and twelve church communities[1]. Based on 2016 ABS data, 22.6% of the population within the Diocese identified as Catholic[2].

Central to understanding the social and historical context in which stories from The Quilt of Hope are located, is an appreciation of the central role the Catholic Church played in the social, economic, political and spiritual lives of Catholics.

Upon arrival in Australia, Catholic immigrants sought to establish Catholic communities, the central institutions being churches and schools. Parish priests were held in high esteem. They were the leaders and spiritual guides for the community and retained the legal and financial responsibility for the Catholic schools within the parish.

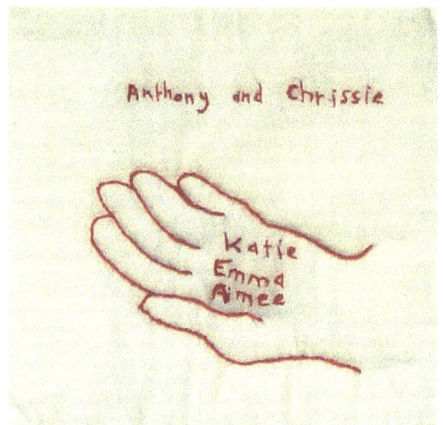

Row 6 Block 44
Made by Lyn Snibson for the Foster family

Row 4 Block 31
Embroidered by Anne Lewis for Helen Last

Parishes were held together by the shared commitment of clergy and laity to provide Catholic education and support the maintenance of the local church. The laity were relied upon for voluntary maintenance, charitable work, fund-raising events and other duties of service to support the functioning of the Church. For many of those whose stories are stitched into the Quilt, the Church was a central part of their lives. It was the community to which they belonged, bonded by the shared faith in God and their Church.

Parishes in this era were often self-contained communities. Partly to avoid the dreaded phenomenon of "mixed marriages" (i.e., where a Catholic married a non-Catholic), endless activities were organised for young Catholic men and women – sporting competitions, dances, balls, picnics, and adult education opportunities.

The hierarchical structure of the Church was well understood by all. The Bishop was the head, the parish priests the local "bosses", supported by curates, followed by religious brothers and sisters. The laity were well and truly at the bottom of the pyramid, however valued they were for fund-raising and other support services. There was never any pretence that the Church was a democracy. Decisions were firmly in the hands of the celibate clergy. Many of the clergy were treated with enormous respect, at times fear, and often with affection and welcomed into parishioners homes and families.

Generations of Catholic families accepted this hierarchical structure unquestioningly and understood the expectations and practices within their faith. The parish priests were the all-knowing, all-seeing representatives of God. They were not to be questioned, for questioning them was questioning God. It was an honour to serve *Father* and have him take an interest in the family.

1960s Vatican II: hope for change

The Second Vatican Council, known as Vatican II, was held in Vatican City between 1962 and 1965. Created by Pope John XXIII, the purpose of the Council was the "modernisation of the Church after 20 centuries of life"[3].

Thousands of bishops and other religious leaders were called to the Vatican City and in his opening speech to the Council, the Pope stated that, "It is absolutely vital that the Church shall never for an instant lose sight of that sacred patrimony of truth inherited from the Fathers. But it is equally necessary for her to keep up to date with the changing conditions of this modern world."[4]

There was much optimism across the Catholic community that genuine change within their Church would occur out of Vatican II. In the end, the main changes put into practice reduced themselves to turning the altar around to face the congregation, changing the saying of Mass to the vernacular rather than Latin, and the fact that women no longer had to cover their hair in Church. These changes did not reflect any significant shift in existing doctrine or practices on topics such as celibacy, contraception, and greater involvement of the laity in the Church.

The anticipated revolutionary shift did not eventuate as the changes that really mattered were not realised. Instead, many Catholics were left with little hope of seeing genuine transformation within their Church.

Following Vatican II, in most churches the clergy continued to maintain the financial, social, political, and spiritual power across the congregations. As the faithful continued to perform services and duties to support their local parish and schools, we now know that children were being sexually abused by the clergy they trusted within their communities. We now know that the Church they were dedicated to and held faith in was actively covering up this abuse and shifting perpetrators from parish to parish. One reason this was able to continue was that at this time any criticism of the clergy was viewed as disloyal to the Church. For most Catholics, it was simply inconceivable that a representative of God would harm children in any way. Children were forced into silence by the fear of not being believed and for many this fear was well founded.

1980s –1990s Isolated Cases: The Church Responds

Despite a reluctance to criticise priests, there were rumours throughout the 1980s of 'inappropriate behaviour' amongst some of them. Carmel Moloney (see chapter 4) recalls hearing comments such as "father touching inappropriately" and this being explained as "frolicking" and "horse play". The Catholic community did not have any comprehension or understanding of child sexual abuse or the meaning of the word paedophile. "We heard rumours", said Carmel, "but you didn't think it was sexual abuse."

Row 2 Block 10
Maker Unknown

Row 5 Block 34
Made by Lyn Snibson

By the 1990s, significant media and public attention began to be given to cases of clerical child sexual abuse in other parts of the world. In 1993, the Catholic community in the Ballarat Diocese was shocked by the revelations that, Father Gerald Ridsdale (a now laicised Catholic priest), had been charged and then jailed a year later for multiple accounts of child sexual abuse. This was the beginning of the unveiling of countless horrors inflicted upon hundreds of children by this one priest. The role the Church played in covering up his actions and moving him around the diocese would be revealed decades later. Advocacy groups such as *In Good Faith* and *Broken Rites* formed to support victims coming forward and provide voice to the issue. The formation of Broken Rites unearthered a multitude of credible cases that contributed to charges against clerics such as Father Gerald Ridsdale, Brother Robert Best, Brother Ted Dowlan and Brother Stephen Frances Farrell[5].

The Church was under increasing pressure from both government and the community to respond to the growing number of reports of historical child sexual abuse. Internally, the Church had been updating its protocols earlier in the decade; and the Australian Catholic Bishops Conference took out a 'special issues' liability insurance policy with the Catholic Church Insurance Limited. This would appear to be a strategic move to ensure the protection of assets in anticipation of cases that would inevitably emerge. Further to this, the 'Melbourne Response' scheme was announced in 1996 (also known as 'The Pell Response'), focusing only on the Melbourne Archdiocese. The 'Towards Healing' program for all Australian Catholic dioceses was established in the same year.

Both programs would later attract immense criticism as it became clear that in handling matters internally, the primary goal of the Church was to minimise scrutiny and manage information provided from victims by the Church's lawyers. The process of compensation was viewed as essentially a payoff for silence with many victims reporting being given little choice but to sign agreements waiving their right for any further action to be taken. After they had accepted low levels of compensation, the matters were seen to be finalised as far as the Church was concerned. Victims were not encouraged to take allegations to the police for criminal investigation, which meant that the Church could avoid further exposure and tarnishing its reputation in the wider community.

The congregations were assured that these were isolated cases and that the Church was taking action to address the injustices and was providing support to victims. Whilst shocked at what they were seeing in the media, many held the faith that their Church was doing what they said they were doing. They were unaware of the emotional and financial battles victims and their families were facing in seeking justice or of the tireless work of advocates to be heard by the Church.

Row 2 Block 13
Unknown Maker

Row 1 Block 5
Truth & Peace, Unknown

Those living through the experience knew different. They found the Church they had been connected to was not one of care and support but rather one of distance and brutal adversarial processes. For most, the Church's starting point was disbelief in the victims. The burden of proof lay squarely with the victims. As they fought to be believed, they relived the trauma of events that had occurred decades ago. Victims were silenced with nominal compensation. Whistleblowers were stonewalled, threatened, and generally brushed aside.

2000-2022 A slow and painful awakening

The magnitude of the problem and depth of depravity emerged in the subsequent years as advocates relentlessly fought for justice and government inquiries revealed a truth that was beyond comprehension. Victims continued to come forward to report what had happened to them and further cases against clergy were brought to court. As multiple offenders faced convictions, Church claims that these were isolated cases were seen to be far from the truth.

Media programs continued to bring attention to the cover up by the Church and following evidence presented to government inquiries, the extent to which the Church had knowledge of not only Ridsdale's offending but of multiple clerical offenders was revealed. Offending clergy had been transferred between parishes, resulting in more children being abused. The focus of Church authorities, however, continued to be protecting the reputation of the Church.

Government Inquiries

Victorian inquiries

In January 2011, the Victorian government announced the *Protecting Victoria's Vulnerable Children Inquiry*. It aimed to investigate systemic problems in Victoria's child protection system. The Cummins Inquiry[6] as it became known, identified concerns regarding the handling of criminal child abuse in religious organisations in Victoria and recommended that a formal investigation be conducted.

This led in turn to the Victorian *Inquiry into the handling of child abuse by religious and other non-government organisations* held in 2012. The final publication, *Betrayal of Trust*[7], released in November 2013, reverberated throughout the Catholic communities, particularly across the Diocese of Ballarat. As noted by Lyn Snibson,

> *We stood in the rain on the steps of Parliament House and many wept with relief.*

For those inside the House on that day in November 2013 and for others later watching television news, the list of towns and cities named as places where children had been abused was shocking.

Based on Broken Rites research and the evidence presented to the Committee in the Ballarat Diocese, towns affected by child abuse perpetrated by Catholic clergy included (in alphabetical order): Apollo Bay, Ararat, Ballarat, Camperdown, Colac, Edenhope, Inglewood, Hamilton, Horsham, Maryborough, Mildura, Mortlake, Ouyen, Penshurst, Portland, Port Fairy, Sea Lake, Swan Hill, Tatyoon, Terang, Warrnambool, Wendouree. Many of these towns contained numerous victims and numerous offenders.[8]

Betrayal of Trust was the first time many Victorians were presented with direct accounts of the horrific events endured by those who shared their truths with the Committee. Attending the public hearings, John Cleary[9] recalled the moment of shock on the first day of the inquiry, "I went there to defend my Church and left without a Church".

New South Wales inquiry – Hunter Valley Region

At the same time as the Victorian Inquiry was taking place, a public meeting was held in Newcastle calling for a Royal Commission into clerical child sexual abuse. It was at this meeting in November 2012 that former Hunter Valley region Detective Chief Inspector Peter Fox felt an overwhelming need to speak up upon hearing a speaker use the words "All that is necessary for the triumph of evil is that good men do nothing". He writes:

> *His words sent me reeling. They really were talking about me. I knew, and I was doing nothing. My excuses suddenly vanished. There would be a price for what I was about to do, but I refused to think about it. I just wanted the evil to stop. I couldn't remain seated any longer. No more excuses.[10]*

This moment was the first of multiple times Peter Fox would allege the Catholic Church was covering up for paedophile priests, silencing investigations, and destroying crucial evidence to avoid prosecution. On the 9th November, he wrote to Barry O'Farrell, the then NSW Premier requesting further investigations be undertaken. That evening, he appeared on *Lateline* and revealed what he knew to a national audience. It was a truth later echoed by former Mildura detective Dennis Ryan in his book *Unholy Trinity* [11] published the following year.

The day after the *Lateline* program was aired, the NSW Premier announced a Special Commission of Inquiry into police handling of abuse by Catholic Church clergy in NSW's Hunter Valley region.

Royal Commission

With the Victorian inquiry underway and the announcement of the Special Commission of Inquiry in the NSW Hunter Valley Region, the then Prime Minister Julia Gillard, announced the Royal Commission into Institutional Responses to Child Sexual Abuse on 12th November 2012.

Commencing in 2013, the Royal Commission held 57 formal public hearings. Over 400 days of hearings, it heard evidence from 1,200 witnesses about the reality of child sexual abuse within institutions. The case studies, released in 2017, focused on "how institutions have responded to allegations and proved instances of child sexual abuse".[12]

For those in the Ballarat Diocese, the *Report of Case Study No.28 Catholic Church authorities in Ballarat* [13], revealed further damning information about their Diocese and exposed the active cover up of child sexual abuse by their Church leaders. For those bearing witness to the evidence presented throughout the public hearings, it was more agonising knowledge of the actions of their Church.

Clerical Power and Pastoral Care. How did it come to this?

***

The Quilt of Hope was made during a time when what we now know to be true about the extent of clerical child sexual abuse was disbelieved by many. It was an unfathomable and gruesome truth that was unbearable to face, particularly for those dedicated to their faith and Church.

It is within this social and historical context the story of the Quilt of Hope is located. It began with a phone call received by Carmel in 2011 when the issue of clerical child sexual abuse was no longer whispered conversations, sordid rumours or sporadic media reports. It was the lived experience of a life-long friend.

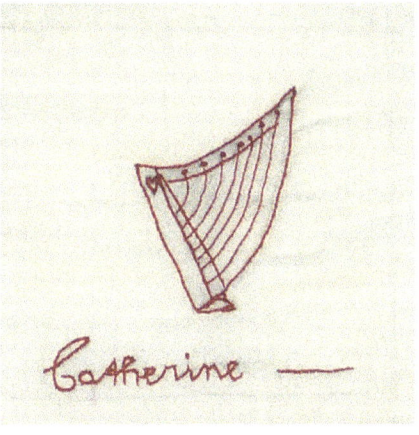

Row 10 Block 76
Unknown

Row 3 Block 23
Made by Catherine Arthur

Endnotes

1   https://www.ballarat.catholic.org.au/
2   National Centre for Pastoral Research. (2019). "Diocesan Social Profile": Based on the 2016 Australian Census. Australia: National Centre for Pastoral Research. (2019). Retrieved from https://ncpr.catholic.org.au/wp-content/uploads/2019/09/Ballarat_2016-Diocesan-Profile.pdf

3   https://www.carroll.edu/mission-catholic-identity/second-vatican-council
4   Ibid.
5   Broken Rites has been researching the cover-up of sexual abuse in the Catholic Church since 1993. Refer to http://www.brokenrites.org.au
6   P. Cummins, D. Scotty, OAM, & B. Scales AO, (2012). Report of the protecting Victoria's vulnerable children inquiry. Available at http://childprotectioninquiry.archive.vic.gov.au/
7   Parliament of Victoria. (2013). Inquiry into the handling of child abuse by religious and other non-government organisations. Available at https://www.parliament.vic.gov.au/340-fcdc/inquiry-into-the-handling-of-child-abuse-by-religious-and-other-organisations.
8   Snibson, L. (2016). Moving Towards Justice: A local public response to the revelation of historical clerical sexual abuse in the Diocese of Ballarat. [Unpublished] (p21)
9   Conversation in 2018 with John Cleary, a member of Moving Towards Justice
10 Fox, P. (2019). Walking towards thunder. Sydney: Hachette Australia. (p12)
11 Ryan, D. & Hoysted, P. (2018). Unholy Trinity (2nd ed). Crows Nest: Allen & Unwin.
12 http://www/childabuseroyalcommission.gov.au
13 Royal Commission into institutional responses to child sexual abuse. (2015). Case study 28 transcript: Catholic Church authorities in Ballarat. Retrieved from http://www/childabuseroyalcommission.gov.au

Chapter 2

Moving Towards Justice

"Never doubt that a small group of thoughtful committed citizens can change the world: indeed, it's the only thing that ever has."
Margaret Mead 1978

It is not often that the actions of small groups are documented in detail; in many cases their stories are simply lost in time. The journey of Moving Towards Justice (MTJ), a grassroots group formed in 2011, was written in 2016 by Lyn Snibson, a founding member and secretary of MTJ.[1] This document provides the narrative of actions taken by a small group of people against an institution with immense political, social, economic, and spiritual power. It was a fight they took up over ten years. As they said to me, "We didn't realise it was that significant, we just rolled with each bit".

In her preface within the document, Heather O'Connor noted that it is;

the story of a group of lay people and their friends coming to terms with the enormity of a social evil perpetrated by those whom they had once held in esteem. For many in the Church, the issue of abuse was the catalyst for their first serious questioning of the hierarchy, and not infrequently, meant incurring the anger of fellow parishioners, and in some cases, the anger of their families.

What follows is an abridged version of their account to ensure the actions of this group are not lost in history and can be shared to a wider audience. Written over 18 months before the findings of the Royal Commission were released in November 2017, none of the members could have foreseen the further revelations and ugly truth that emerged in the subsequent five years following the termination of the formal incorporation of their group.[2]

While MTJ may no longer exist as a formal entity, it still operates on an informal level. The shared journey of its members forged strong bonds of friendship and they continue to support each other and those around them.

The following excerpt covers the period from 2011 until 2016. Reflections of what has come to pass since that time has been provided by Lyn Snibson, the author of the MTJ story.

***

Beginnings

In 2011, sexual abuse in the Catholic Church took on a personal face for a small group of parishioners at St Columba's in Ballarat North. Carmel, a member of the Parish Bereavement Team, was made aware of the sexual abuse suffered in childhood by Michael, son of her friend Margot. Michael's life had been difficult for decades before his family finally discovered his terrible secret: as a child he had been the victim of a predatory Christian Brother.

For Carmel, the revelation was deeply shocking and she was compelled to find a way to attempt to bring comfort to Margot and to Michael. Those of us who teamed with her that week to plan a service of healing had no inkling of what we were to discover over the next four years or of what would be required of each of us.

Row 8 Block 58
Maker Unknown

Row 1 Block 4
Maker Unknown

As ordinary parishioners, our awareness of church related sexual abuse had begun slowly. Ballarat priest Gerald Ridsdale went to jail in 1994. Those of us who noticed at all were led to believe that victims were being looked after. Bishop Peter Connors published a letter to the parishes in 2007 apologising to victims. There were rumblings about misconduct but, on the whole, things were kept quiet. Most of us had no real understanding of the scope of the problem or, more importantly, the lifelong consequences for the victims, their families and communities. We wonder now why we parishioners and the broader community failed to engage with the issue.

Initial response

Each of us who became associated with Carmel's initiative to reach out to Margot and Michael, through her, began to really listen, to ask questions of Church leaders and communities, and to read widely.

Chrissie Foster's book *Hell on the way to heaven*[3] had just been published. This gave an appalling insight into church related paedophilia. It also provided us with the terrible awareness of what had happened to Anthony and Chrissie's two daughters when, as very young children, they had been sexually abused by parish priest Kevin O'Donnell at Oakleigh.

Anthony and Chrissie Foster's experience, as parents of victims, highlighted for us the incomprehensible responses they received from the Catholic Church over the years they struggled to find justice for their family. It was hard for us to believe that our Church could react in such a seemingly callous way; and that George Pell, who was born and had grown up to become a priest in Ballarat, had allegedly played a significant role in that injustice.

The media reported policeman Kevin Carson's findings exposing Father Ridsdale and Christian Brothers Robert Best and Edward Dowlan [now known as Bales] as paedophiles. We heard that the sexual abuse of children in the Diocese of Ballarat by church personnel might also be linked to over three dozen suspected suicides.

Once we began to speak out about the shocking things we were learning, victims, families and others started to make contact with us to tell of their experiences and what they knew. A bookseller from Yackandandah, Carmel's friend Mary, undertook to provide our group with the information gradually coming through in new writings. *Unholy trinity: the hunt for the paedophile priest Monsignor John Day* by Denis Ryan and Peter Hoysted[4]; Christopher Geraghty's *Dancing with the devil: a journey from the pulpit to the bench*[5] and *Potiphar's wife: the Vatican's secret and child sex abuse* by Kieran Tapsell[6] were some of the titles circulated amongst us. To say we felt betrayed by Catholic Church leaders would be an understatement.

The personal knowledge we were gaining and the reading made available to us, finally brought home the extent of the problem. It helped us to understand the extreme damage wrought upon the victims and families over decades. We were drawn together to seek further support from each other and from church and community members who were sympathetic and who might join us to take the issue further.

Practical response

A number of us met at the tearooms above the historical waiting room for coaches at the Ballarat New Cemetery, to plan the proposed service for all who had been impacted by church related abuse. We called on a bereavement specialist and included mothers of victims. There was hurt but also hope at that meeting but, as the weeks passed, we began to see that a service was not going to be enough. As it happened, it never eventuated.

Owners of a local tavern offered a meeting room, coffee and privacy. We asked to use the facility for an afternoon of music. Professional musicians offered their services and contributed to a happy and generous day for victims we had come to know, families and supporters. We began to understand that justice was needed, not charity.

People continued to contact us to talk about their family experiences. Some felt that the church was more concerned about protecting its own reputation than helping victims of childhood sexual abuse by paedophiles within the Catholic churches and schools.

Our parish priest had warned us to be careful; that we could be hurt, as he had been, when he reached out to help victims in previous years. This, in fact, later proved to be prophetic. We were very aware, also, that we risked hurting him, and other priests we held in high regard, by trying to bring the issue before all parishioners.

Some of us felt we could no longer continue to support the Church and were drawing back from the heavy involvement we had with the Parish while others continued to play a full part in its life.

Moving Towards Justice forms

In 2012 the Cummins Report had been released *(see Chapter 1)*. This identified the need for a formal investigation into the processes by which religious organisations respond to the criminal abuse of children by religious personnel within their organisations[7].

This in turn resulted in the convening of the Family and Community Development Committee of the Victorian Government to undertake an inquiry into the handling of child abuse by religious and other non-government organisations.

In August, 2012, an information forum was held at Midlands Golf Club in Ballarat. It had been convened by groups, predominantly from Melbourne, who were already assisting victims. Their purpose was to provide information on the preparation of submissions from victims to be presented to the recently announced Victorian State Government Inquiry into Handling of Child Abuse by Religious and Other Non-Government Organisations.

This meeting gave us the opportunity to meet victims and to see that we were not alone in our endeavours. The Ballarat Centre Against Sexual Assault (CASA), Melbourne Victims Collective, For the Innocents (FTI) and Sexual Assault Victims' Advocates, Melbourne (SAVAs) all contributed to the day.

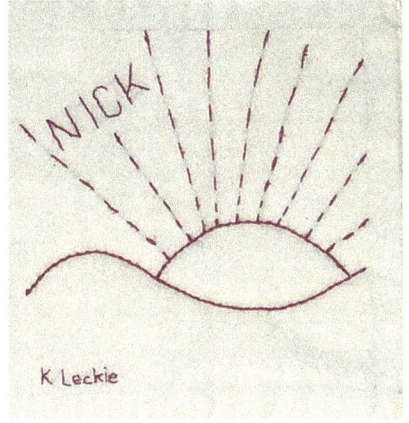

Row 1 Block 6
Maker Unknown

Row 10 Block 78
Anonymous maker for a friend

It became obvious to us that we needed people with some influence in the church and community to help to bring about action. By December 2012 there were about thirty of us concerned enough to meet regularly. These included a retired State politician Frank Sheehan who was to become our chairperson, a former bank manager, businessmen, teachers, nurses, psychologists, an ABC radio presenter, religious sisters and priests and two retired solicitors.

The majority of us were retired and most, at that time, were practising Catholics. The composition of the Committee was important as we needed professional expertise. There were two givens: the vulnerability of those we hoped to support and the power of the institution we planned to challenge.

Three Ballarat East Sisters of Mercy gave the group a legitimacy with other parishioners and with Church leadership that we may not otherwise have had. The Sisters gave generous and constant support in many ways including financial, administrative and a room in which to gather each month.

Four men, all middle aged, were to join us. Each was a victim of sexual abuse by priests or Christian Brothers in this Diocese. Coming to know these men helped us to realize that victims are individuals having different ideas on what was required to redress the crimes committed against them.

We came to understand the toll advocacy and care of others was taking on survivors who were making a public stand. In the process, they were subjecting themselves and their families to public and media scrutiny, the apparent indifference of the church communities and the ire of Catholic Church hierarchy.

Working with others

We began to connect with Melbourne groups *For the Innocents* and *In Good Faith*. Through our contact with them, including attendance at some of their meetings, our own knowledge was increased and we gained confidence from the fact that we were not alone as lay people trying to support victims in the Ballarat Diocese.

While this was happening farmer and businessman John, one of our members, had begun to make contact with Ann Ryan in Warrnambool. He arranged to meet Ann and to talk to her about her experience as a teacher librarian in the Catholic school in Mortlake and the subsequent battles she fought with the church on behalf of boys sexually abused by Gerald Ridsdale, the Parish Priest for some of the time Ann worked there *(see Chapter 7)*.

John found Ann and Garry Ryan a little hesitant to meet him at first. They didn't know why he would be interested in what had happened in the Western District nearly thirty years before. They were tired of the fight too; it had taken its toll over many years. Eventually, however, Ann was encouraged to take her story to the Victorian Inquiry.

Bishop Peter Connors of Ballarat said in his evidence at the Inquiry that Ann Ryan was the only one who had tried to do something about what had been happening in the school at Mortlake. We now know that Sister of Mercy Kate McGrath, who was principal of the Catholic parish primary school at Mortlake at that time, had also approached Bishop Mulkearns but to no avail.

Ann and Kate both made statements to the Hearings of the Royal Commission into Institutional Responses to Child Sexual Abuse. Ann and Garry Ryan have become admired and loved friends of many of the Moving Towards Justice members.

In October, 1993, Ann had sent a letter to twenty of the priests of the Diocese of Ballarat (refer to Appendix A). It also went to Bishop Mulkearns and to several of Ann's close friends. If we had believed that nobody had been aware of the sexual abuse issue in the Church, seeing this letter was a sad awakening.

In it Ann explains her pain and frustration that the hierarchy and priests remained silent about the sexual abuse committed on children of Mortlake by Gerald Ridsdale. She asks *'How can we truly live with ourselves, as church, in such a thundering silence of injustice and ugliness?'*

In her letter, Ann relates in detail what parents had told her had happened at St. Colman's Catholic Primary school in Mortlake. She also writes in that letter of the response of Bishop Mulkearns to two families who between them had five sons who had been sexually abused by the priest: *'...they were made to feel like the criminal and the Bishop remained unmoved until [one mother] threatened police action.'*

Ann included in the letter her suggestions for actions for healing within the Church. Of the priests and the Bishop sent the letter, only three or four responded. And there, listed at the end, were the names of those to whom the letter was sent. To our dismay it included names of many of the priests we knew so well.

What had begun for us with the story of one man, Margot's son Michael, was being revealed as an epidemic.

The Story of the Quilt of Hope

There was some disquiet in local parish churches as newspapers and television had begun to report on the impending Victorian Inquiry. It was not unusual to hear parishioners and priests blame the media for attacking the Catholic Church. Many Catholics did not want to know about the abuse. *'If it happened at all it was a long time ago'* and *'Why can't they just get over it.'* Many times we heard the refrain, *'They [the victims] are just looking for money'*.

In the meantime we continued to offer practical support to anyone recommended to us. Ideas abounded. Some were implemented and some discarded as we were guided by members who were also victims.

An early initiative was to attempt to bring together an associated group of professional counsellors and other health providers who might be willing to provide services, subsidized by MTJ, to victims and others impacted by church related sexual abuse.

Georgina Anderson, a Ballarat based counsellor, worked tirelessly on our behalf to organise such a group. Her generosity and dedication towards victims was ultimately in vain for two reasons. Firstly, we had underestimated the level of psychological care being provided by CASA and the stake that body had in receiving government funding for their services.

The second reason for the ultimate demise of this initiative was the clear preference our member religious sisters and priests had for Catholic practitioners. Some were concerned that the sexual abuse issue not be handled by people outside of the church; some were not confident that the level of expertise required was available. Victims and families known to us found this to be unacceptable. For many it would be too painful to re-engage with those still closely aligned with the church and there was the added complication that those available to provide counselling may also have been involved with counselling of the perpetrators of abuse.

The Victorian Inquiry

It seemed that we should take a public stand and two submissions were tended by members of our group. Carmel's sister agreed to provide advice and practical help with the writing of some of the submissions from victims and families. The submissions of our members described the culture of the family and the church from the 1960's and expressed the shock we'd experienced in what we had discovered had taken place under the bishops' watch.

In October 2012 the Victorian Inquiry Hearings began. Our group members travelled to Parliament House in Spring Street, Melbourne, on many occasions, both to inform ourselves and to support witnesses. It was heart-warming for us to be accepted so readily and generously by victims. We spent time talking together on the train journey to and from Melbourne, learning more of what had happened to these people when they were still young boys, and comparing notes on how we believed the day's proceedings had gone.

The Victorian Inquiry had, for the first time, provided a place and an opportunity for the victims to tell their stories, to be truly heard and believed. It made public the shameful behaviour of those who had sexually abused children entrusted to their care. It highlighted the abysmal response of the Catholic Church, using its power, influence and money to defend the reputation of the Church and its wealth.

Towards Healing

Towards Healing had been set up by the bishops and leaders of religious groups in Australia in 1996 to deal with the issue of paedophilia within the Catholic Church community. The Victorian Inquiry brought to light major flaws in Towards Healing and the Melbourne Response. We had witnessed, at close hand, shortcomings in the process of Towards Healing. One of our members had been active in its earlier days and suggested that we invite Kerry Buchecker from Towards Healing to attend a meeting so that we could learn more about this Church initiative to deal with the problem. Kerry brought with her copies of the Towards Healing manual and explained the process involved once an allegation of sexual abuse had been made to them.

Moving Towards Justice evolved from a small group of people who couldn't believe what we were hearing about 'our church'. When we began to ask church officials about what had been done, and what else needed to be done to reach out to those impacted by church related sexual abuse, we were embarrassed at their recalcitrance.

We were also frustrated that others couldn't see what we could see: that the leaders of the Church were dragging their feet instead of proactively offering compensation and redress to survivors. We had come to see, at close quarters, that Towards Healing was anything but proactive.

Row 8 Block 57
Made by Lyn Snibson

Row 2 Block 9

The Royal Commission

The Royal Commission into Institutional Responses to Child Sexual Abuse was announced by the Federal Labour government led by Julia Gillard on November 12th, 2012. In January 2015, Moving Towards Justice was contacted by an investigator who had been looking at our website and requested a meeting. Following this meeting we were asked if we would be willing to provide a submission to the Royal Commission. The Public Hearing, scheduled for May, was to focus on community impacts of the sexual abuse in the Ballarat Diocese.

To interact with the Inquiry was not an easy decision. The lay people amongst us were concerned for the clerical and religious on our Committee and any impact it might have on them. As it happened, the Mercy Sisters, with courage and generosity, urged us on and we provided information to the Royal Commission around our reasons for forming as a group and advocating for victims.

The Commission was interested in our responses to questions about our Catholic and local communities: whether the Church was co-operating with us in looking for solutions; what we had achieved that was of benefit to victims; the impact that church related sexual abuse had on the parishes and city; and reasons we could identify that might explain why it was so prevalent in the Ballarat Diocese.

Our submission was seen to be of value and we were asked if a representative of the group would be prepared to make a Statement and to appear before Justice McClellan and Commissioners. Moving Towards Justice President, Frank Sheehan, agreed to do this with the help of the Secretary, Lyn Snibson. Together they met with an investigator and a lawyer from the Commission who prepared the Statement with them. Issues addressed were personalized so that they pertained to Frank's experience. This was necessary to suit the requirement of the Public Hearings and the submission previously given was tabled at the time Frank appeared before Justice McClellan.

Frank was able to elucidate the culture in which he grew up as a young person involved in many aspects of church life. He described the hopes and dreams newly introduced to Catholics at the time of Vatican II in the 1960's and '70's, and the disappointment felt when reforms were shied away from and failed to materialize. Frank represented the voice of many when he said that sexual abuse in the church and Catholic schools would have been unimaginable and unbelievable to him until it finally surfaced in about 2011. He needed to look up the meaning of 'paedophile' in his dictionary and, at this time, he was a man in his mid-seventies.

In speaking of the response of and impact on the community of Ballarat, Frank noted that often, when the issue of child sexual abuse arose, parishioners gathered around priests to try to protect them. He identified a disconnect whereby Catholics talk about how hard it has been on priests who haven't offended but little was said about how hard it has been on victims.

His statement concluded with the observation that he, personally, was embarrassed and shocked that child sexual abuse has happened in his church and also annoyed that parishioners were not properly informed. Frank also stated that he was ashamed of the response made to this issue by Church leaders.

He concluded

'As a parishioner, I felt as though we were betrayed and thrown into the deep end of discovery. We could and should have been told about what happened, and we should have been involved in some sort of pro-active response initiated by the Church leadership.'

The Royal Commission investigator had told us that we would be allocated a solicitor for the Public Hearing and that Counsellors would be available should we need them. She said that she did not want to see Moving Towards Justice damaged in any way. This was puzzling to us as we believed that we had a good relationship with survivors, advocates and agencies. We were, however, to receive public criticism from some victims and advocates in their witness statements.

The need to communicate truth to parishioners

Part of our response to church related child abuse was to try to bring the issue to prominence within the parishes so that others might understand the true impact on victims. As the years passed, and the public investigations into institutional responses to allegations of child sexual abuse began, it would be difficult for anyone to be unaware of the shameful history of this Diocese.

The challenge is for parishioners to take responsibility for the failings of the church in past decades and to find ways to support survivors. We have seen, sadly, that children of some survivors may also have been disadvantaged, leading to another generation of those impacted.

Personal impact

Church and the idea of Christian faith and religious practice remains strong for some of those who became part of the team. Some, however, have left the Church; some intend to do so. Some struggle between the thought that it would be helpful to try to make changes from within the Church community and the thought of just giving it all away.

Many in Moving Towards Justice had shared a faith evolving from Vatican II. Some had a friendship reaching back to the 1960's when they were educated and encouraged by priests ahead of their time. As lay people they had been taught Cardinal Cardjin's principle of 'see, judge, and act' and had trusted church leaders to act in the best interests of people.

Some of us will never again see the Church as we have in the past; some leaders have lost our trust and respect. The weakness they displayed historically by not standing up for the vulnerable in an honest and public way has resulted in too much pain for too many families.

We 'tried and true' Catholics have each reacted differently to what we now know.

One parishioner, motivated to become a member of Moving Towards Justice, wrote a letter to the Parish Priest in May, 2013. In it she expresses grief at the loss of trust experienced in coming to terms with what had occurred

> *...Last night I attended the Parish Stewardship Program and heard of the Parish's need for funding over the next three years. As I sat in that assembly, my gaze scanning the wonderful community gathered there, I felt an overwhelming sadness that I no longer feel that I can commit unreservedly to our shared life.*
>
> *Less than eighteen months ago such a thought would have been unimaginable to me. My life over the last twenty five years as a converted Catholic has been rich and fulfilled with treasured friendships, learning and opportunities to grow as a person.*
>
> *...On Monday I think I was the only person from [this parish] and only one of four from Ballarat to attend the Parliamentary Inquiry in Melbourne to hear our Bishop's response to the handling of child abuse in the diocese. The other three people consisted of two Sisters of Mercy and a parishioner more loosely connected to the parish.*
>
> *The evidence I heard was shocking, and closely resembled what has been written about the same situation in other countries.*
>
> *……. you said at the meeting last night, quite rightly, that the church has taken a battering. You have also previously said, from the pulpit, that the media must carry some blame. May I offer an alternative view?*

> *I see the media as friend in this case, not 'the enemy'. The reporting of the Inquiry each time I have attended has been accurate and fair. It is only through the media that all Catholics might hear the truth of what has been happening in their church. They deserve to know.*

> *… It was not surprising to hear that all we had come to suspect with regard to the movement of paedophile priests around the diocese was true. Our bishops, as in other countries when this has been discovered, pleaded naiveté and the belief that paedophilia is curable. I was pleased when the Committee pointed out that from earliest times in this country it has been a serious criminal offence punishable, in earlier times, by the death penalty. Only a fool could think otherwise. The untold misery caused to some families of the parishes could have been lessened had appropriate action been taken at the time. It is difficult not to feel shame at the high handed attitudes of those who could have prevented further atrocities.*

> *Thomas Keneally, in an article published in 2002, said that his crisis of faith came shortly before he was to be ordained '[It] came from my realization that, behind the compelling mystery of Catholicism, with its foundation in the message of 'Caritas Christi' …lay a cold and largely self-interested corporate institution.'*

> *It is hard to see beyond that at present.*

> *… The result of all of this is that … I struggle to remain in the church. I can't commit to tomorrow let alone three years ………. It has to be wait and see, hoping that Pope Francis is strong enough to make the changes needed in a church gone astray.*

Another member of Moving Towards Justice, reflecting on his experience, wrote:

> *…I believe each of us has been affected in personal ways as a result of our shared experiences within M.T.J. There are really tangible elements of collateral damage or fallout, and personally, I feel the right to claim to be a "victim" in the sense of being let down by the institutional Church. Don't we all? Is it like "tilting at windmills"*

> *to feel that ordinary people, who make up the membership of the church can tackle the Institutional Church to see the need for structural change?*
>
> *...I know we face a huge road block in the defensive stance of many of our clergy, which I believe stems from Vatican policy and the system it controls. Somehow this needs to be worn down - but how? Loud Fence and people like Kevin Dillon and Justin Driscoll need to be affirmed & encouraged. This process of seeking to change public awareness was one of the original objectives we took on board. Is there still a task for us to work for change?*

The challenge is for the whole Church community to accept the reality of the abuse and the extent to which the Church went to protect its own to the detriment of victims. It is not acceptable to blame victims for the discomfort many of the Catholic community feel because of the public airing of this issue.

For Moving Towards Justice members it would not be an exaggeration to say that we were naïve to believe we could find a way forward for victims who could no longer trust anyone because their trust had been so badly betrayed; many with damaged relationships, little self-belief and poor self-esteem.

The crime against them as children has been described as 'soul murder'. We felt compelled to act but found ourselves often out of our depth and lacking skills needed. Victims and families were to teach us we could only contribute in a small way when more was needed and sometimes expected.

At the Annual General Meeting of Moving Towards Justice, held in August 2015, members voted to cease incorporation in December 2015. We planned to meet informally from February 2016 and to continue to provide friendship to those survivors with whom we continue to have a relationship. Our work was not finished, nor were we redundant as an association of like-minded people.

In the Special Resolution notes as part of the rationale to cease incorporation it was recorded that:

The past four years have taken a toll on many of us. We have worked hard for survivors while, at the same time, coming to understand the full impact of what has happened in our Church. Some of us have felt shocked, distressed, and betrayed by the way in which the complaints of abuse were handled by those in power. We have walked an unpopular pathway through the revelations and our push to have the issue addressed. We are four years older and wiser. Have we given enough?

Our work will continue to be taken up by others and we await the findings of the Royal Commission in the hope that the Catholic Church might become a beacon, in acts as well as words, for the wellbeing of those who have carried the impact and burden of child sexual abuse.

17th March, 2016
Lyn Snibson

***

Since the writing of the MTJ journey in 2016, the Catholic Church did not become a beacon Lyn had hoped for. Over the past six years, revelations about the extent of historical clerical child sexual abuse, the cover up and corruption continue to flow into the public realm.

In 2018 I shared dinner with founding MTJ members Lyn Snibson, John Cleary, Mary Darcy and Carmel Moloney along with Mike Parer (Chair/Convenor For the Innocents, FTI) and Father Kevin Murphy. As we spoke about the book, discussions covered multiple topics of what has come to pass, the narrative of the time, and of what may come. What was evident to me was the fatigue felt by the founding members. It had been almost 8 years since they commenced their journey and revelations of the atrocities committed by the Church continued to emerge. As the conversation progressed, I could feel the wave of different emotions experienced as they described the events that unfolded with their awakening to the immoral actions of the Church. I could feel the collective sadness, the collective anger, the collective sense of achievement, and the collective admiration for one another.

Lyn Snibson reflects in 2022 and writes

I lost trust in the institutional church but not in the community of church and deeply respect those who remained in the hope of reforming and healing from within. I had converted to Catholicism in 1989 and was an active member, sometimes bored with it, but never seeing the dark side of the religion. So many good people were church for me. But I saw for myself how the church hierarchy distanced itself from the hurt for which it was responsible. I came to believe that the institutional church exists for itself alone and has forgotten what Christianity represents. It left decent and generous priests and religious sisters trying to find a way forward while 'The Church' put itself above its people and above the law, losing credibility in the process.

I would like to pay tribute to Sister Rita Hayes RSM who died in November, 2016. Rita, a member of MTJ, was a positive and forward looking woman always thinking of ways to make a difference in the lives of survivors of abuse.

The journey they commenced together transformed their lives and created a unique bond between them that may not have occurred but for the need to act when learning what they had discovered.

***

Frank Sheehan, an esteemed statesman, community member, and friend, passed away on the 5th May 2021. As the President of MTJ, he played a critical leadership role and as was the case with others in the group, could not remain silent as revelations of clerical child sexual abuse emerged. Frank was admired by many and upon his passing, the following tribute was written by Paul

Tatchell, and approved by Frank's wife Rosalie for inclusion in this book.

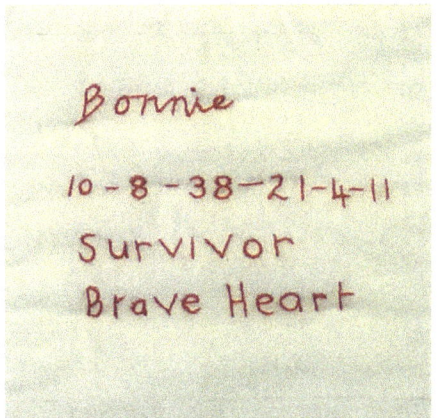

Row 10 Block 75
Made by Lyn Snibson

Row 4 Block 28
Made by Catherine Arthur for
Fr Kevin Dillon

Frank

It's not often that the City of Ballarat goes into mourning; but the loss of Frank Sheehan sent ripples far and wide; Frank epitomised the perfect blend of humility, common sense and selflessness.

Frank set the bar in public life, not just the standard but a code for representation in its purist of forms. Frank's holistic perception of justice knew no boundaries, Frank's light shined brightly over the Bushel measured by calm.

The voice of reason within the unreasonable, never to take a backward step using passive reasoning to march forward in the pursuit of fairness and equity. A velvet sledgehammer driven by integrity, not bluster.

Frank stood for those that could barely stand and fought for those that couldn't fight for themselves. The there was no sand box too deep, or bridge to far.

Frank's commitment to the working class is reflected in the constant evolution of protectionism by policy; Frank pioneered and drove the work safe policies through Spring Street often taken for granted.

Frank stood firmly behind, beside and in front of the working class, determined without fear nor favour, not for recognition, but to resolve, the unresolved.

Feared only by those that had something to fear; Frank followed the footsteps of the fisherman, through faith and forgiveness. Frank may have been drawn to the left, but only if it was for the right reasons.

Frank never lost his faith or his faith in people; the eternal optimist for good and not evil, all weighted by reality not perceptions.

The current band of politicians could learn a lot from Frank's legacy; "put the people first, politics is just the tool".

Frank's drive and enthusiasm within the Moving Towards Justice group, was indicative of Frank's commitment in bridging the gap between victims of injustice and practical reform.

Frank was tireless in his commitment to lift the dark clouds that had engulfed his beloved Ballarat, Frank did what Frank did best, brought people to the table. His infectious smile masked his dogged determination.

A leader not just by definition but by example.

The loss of Ballarat's favourite son will be hard felt; but Frank's spirit will live on in all touched by his influence; every time I had the privilege of speaking with Frank, I walked away wanting to be a better person.

Frank Sinatra may well have sung about doing it "My Way" Frank Sheehan simply did it his!

Paul Tatchell
May 2021

Endnotes

1 Snibson, L. (2016). *Moving Towards Justice: A local public response to the revelation of historical clerical sexual abuse in the Diocese of Ballarat.* [Unpublished]
2 Ibid. (p7)
3 Foster, C. & Kennedy, P. (2011). *Hell on the way to heaven.* Melbourne: Bantam Australia.
4 Ryan, D. & Hoysted, P. (2013). *Unholy Trinity.* Melbourne: Allen & Unwin.
5 Geraghty, C. (2012). *Dancing with the devil: a journey from the pulpit to the bench.* Richmond, Victoria: Spectrum Publications.
6 Tapsell, K. (2014). *Potiphar's wife: the Vatican's secret and child sex abuse.* Hindmarsh, SA: ATF Press.
7 Report of the protecting Victoria's vulnerable children inquiry (2012) Available at http://childprotectioninquiry.archive.vic.gov.au/

Chapter 3

The Quilt of Hope

"It is the histories of these many people, where the needle becomes the pen...the quilt becomes the carrier of messages for many."[1]
Annette Gero

The Quilt of Hope contributes to the vast collection of quilts that capture significant historical moments and add to the patchwork of our social history. It follows in the tradition of textiles that have been used for various practical, decorative, teaching, and symbolic purposes. Serving not only the everyday needs of people, quilts also play major roles in the social, economic, and religious lives of communities. They powerfully express both individual and collective voices.

Textiles and the vehicle of sewing have been used to express stories of protest, memory, identity, power, and politics over centuries and across cultures. As eloquently phrased by Clare Hunter in her book *Threads of Life*:

Sewing is a visual language. It has a voice. It has been used by people to communicate something of themselves—their history, beliefs, prayers and protests ... But it is not a monologue, it is part of a conversation, a dialogue, a correspondence only fully realised once it is seen and its messages read ... As a shared language, needlework transmits—through techniques, coded symbols, fabrics and colour— the unedited stories of not just women, but often of those marginalised by oppression and prejudice. [2]

Within the context of clerical child sexual abuse, the LOUD FENCE movement is one of great significance using coloured ribbons tied to fences of schools and Churches. The movement began in May 2015 on the front fence of the former St Alipius Boys School site, in Victoria Street, Ballarat. The founders were shocked by evidence presented to the Royal Commission and wanted to take some form of action to show victims and survivors that they were believed and their voices were being heard. Bright coloured ribbons were chosen to create a loud message of support in opposition to the silence that had prevailed for so long.

The simple gesture of tying ribbons has generated worldwide support and provides an accessible way for people to symbolically contribute to the collective voice. The ribbons in themselves are memorial pieces and the assemblage of ribbons provides a powerful visual display of solidarity to ensure the voices are never silenced and events are not forgotten.

The long tradition of quilt making serves to tell the stories of people that would not have been captured in any other form. Australia has a rich heritage of patchwork quilts with many older quilts remaining with the makers' families and passed down to each generation.[3] Quilts of national social and historical significance such as the Rajah Quilt, the Gallipoli Red & White Signature Quilt, and the Changi Quilts (refer to Appendix B for further information) are held in public collections.

Row 4 Block 29
Anonymous maker for a family member

Row 7 Block 51
Maker Uknown

The Quilt of Hope

The Quilt of Hope represents the voices of people abused as children, their families who have spoken up and suffered the consequences of challenging a powerful institution, and the voices of those who care. With every stitch and every block, the Quilt tells a story and creates a patchwork of social history that serves as a memorial piece. It symbolises "the putting together of pieces, one by one, of shattered lives and, in the shared experience of the making, to offer belief, dignity and friendship to those still looking for justice from the Catholic Church"[4].

The Quilt comprises 80 individual embroidered calico blocks which have been sewn together inside a red frame to form a traditional remembrance style patchwork quilt. Each block contains words and/or images that were created by both experienced and novice sewers. In some instances, contributors simply wrote the words and/or image on the block and Beryl, the Quilt maker, embroidered their block with red thread.

Single words are scattered through the Quilt along with messages of hope and prayers. There are the names of a loved one or commemorating someone and various motifs such as hearts, doves, butterflies, and crosses or more individualised images. The eight red doves placed across the Quilt commemorate the countless lives lost to suicide.

Why a Quilt?

In 1988, whilst on holiday in America, Carmel Moloney and I visited the United Nations building in New York and viewed a portion of the AIDS Memorial Quilt on display. It was an emotional and overwhelming experience looking at the large panels containing the names of people who had lost their lives to this misunderstood disease. We felt the love and loss of those that had hand crafted each of the panels.

The AIDS Memorial Quilt was displayed for the first time in 1987 during the National March on Washington advocating for Lesbian and Gay Rights. At that time there were approximately 1,900 panels made from a variety of materials and each measuring 3ft x 6ft, the approximate size of a grave. Thirty-five years later, it is one of the largest quilts in the world with over 48,000 individual memorial panels representing over 94,000 people. Weighing an estimated 54 tons and spanning 1.3 million square feet, it cannot be displayed in its entirety in one place. In recognition of its social significance, it was nominated for a Nobel Peace Prize in 1989[5].

It was from this experience that Carmel drew the inspiration to put forward the idea to create a community quilt as a way for people to express their feelings, acknowledge their loved ones and provide messages to those affected. Members of MTJ involved in the project felt it was a practical way to reach out to people and to create a lasting memorial that gives public recognition to the damage caused by clerical child sexual abuse in the Catholic Church. Lyn Snibson captures their thinking at the time,

From the beginning we recognised the pain parents had suffered. We reasoned that if we couldn't reach victims, we could at least reach out to mothers... The Quilt project was undertaken to bring together, in mutual support, mothers and friends of survivors and to be an enduring symbol of compassion for those it represents.[6]

Row 3 Block 17
Maker Uknown

Row 9 Block 65
Maker Uknown

Creating the Quilt

The Quilt was designed and made by Beryl Andersen, a professional quilt maker with over 40 years of experience. When the idea of making the quilt was suggested, Beryl had no hesitation in recommending it be made in the traditional red and white remembrance style.

To promote the making of the Quilt and invite contributions, letters were sent out across the Ballarat Diocese and were included in various Parish newsletters. The invitation asked:

Can we, together, in constructing the Quilt of Hope, be the glue for each other as we seek the justice and care that is your due?

The cream canvas blocks were provided by Beryl and distributed to those expressing interest. The backing for the Quilt was provided by a Castlemaine haberdashery shop. Space for the group to meet was offered by the Sisters of Mercy in Ballarat who would later create a prayer card to accompany the Quilt.

The first gathering brought together more than a dozen women and additional offers of support came from distant towns. Mothers of victims, religious sisters, members of MTJ, parishioners and quilters took away blocks. They embroidered them specifically for a loved one, for those who had suffered for their efforts to bring justice for victims, or simply to provide a message of compassion. As the blocks began to come back, Beryl commenced the task of assembling and quilting the pieces together to create the Quilt.

It was named the Quilt of Hope to represent "the messages of hope and prayers for healing…also contained within it offer our support and tangible reminder that stories have been heard and that people care."[7]

Completed in September 2014, the Quilt was officially launched a month later in Bermagui, New South Wales. The launch coincided with an event focussing on the celebration of women and the launching of Heather O'Connor's book about the role of women in religion[8].

The travelling Quilt

Following the official launch, the Quilt travelled to various venues around Central and Western Victoria for exhibition. Carmel writes:

> *After the launching of the Quilt, we were invited to different parishes so all who had contributed could share in what had been achieved.*
>
> *The Ballarat Diocese is extensive, covering the Western half of Victoria from the Murray River to the Sea. The journey could only be achieved if we shared the travelling and the time it would take.*

The first public viewing of the Quilt was in the foyer of St Joseph's Catholic Church, Warrnambool in March 2015. Mary Lancaster had organised our visit and had well publicised the event. Father Fitzgerald spoke to parishioners about the Quilt and the Royal Commission and read Bishop Paul Bird's letter. He invited all to stop and view the Quilt and its accompanying slide presentation. After Sunday Mass, many leaving the Church remained, some sat in silence, others engaged in conversation. Each of us, individually, was entrusted with stories of personal experiences from different families.

There were tears too, and the comments written in the visitors' book provided us with further insight into the powerful symbolism of the Quilt. People wrote that it was a great idea that may help to bring some peace; that it evoked sad memories; it is inspiring; and that finally the truth is told. One comment "heard and felt" says it all.

The afternoon brought a steady stream of visitors, many saying that people who had seen the Quilt in the morning had contacted them to suggest that they not miss it. Again, people sat, contemplated and watched the slide show through, often for more than one viewing.

Gradually over several weeks the parishes of Mildura, Casterton, Warrnambool, Edenhope, Hamilton and Colaraine welcomed us, and we had the opportunity to witness and contemplate what Mary Darcy described at our launch as 'the many thousands of small stitches that make up the Quilt of Hope as being insignificant in themselves but a powerful symbol bringing not only the Quilt but its makers and the lives it represents together into one story'

As we had hoped, the Quilt opened hearts and has been a catalyst for revelation and healing.

Weeks later when the Royal Commission hearings were in Ballarat, the Mercy Sisters opened their home at the Victoria Street Convent where the Quilt was displayed in their living room.

In this quiet peaceful space people gathered throughout the days of the hearings ... the silence and reverence were powerful. A visitors' book provided the opportunity for those wishing to record their thoughts. The overwhelming emotion was gratitude.

Recorded in the book, we discovered the names of two mothers, both octogenarians who had travelled from Colac. Their Parish Priest was aware that Father Ridsdale had abused their young children and stole their innocence and impacted on their lives, stealing their future potential for happiness. This Parish Priest had always shown empathy not only with words but by informing them about the Quilt on display and driving them to Ballarat. His kindness and compassion have serviced their faith.

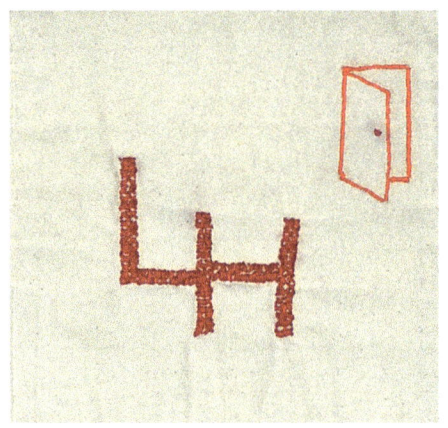

Row 2 Block 14
Made by Lyn Snibson for a victim

Row 7 Block 53
Made by Clare Linnane

As we travelled to different parishes, we became aware that parishioners were finding it difficult to take responsibility for the failings of their church. It was unbearable knowledge – the extent of the abuse was overwhelming.

The visual impact as they sat silently contemplating so many lives and the Red Doves representing the victims who had completed their lives helped open their minds and soften their hearts. Many felt betrayed – some angry, others telling us they were victims let down by an institutional church who cared more about its image and reputation that the pastoral care of the laity.

For those whose lives were represented on the Quilt, there was a sense of relief and gratitude because at least their pain and suffering were acknowledged and believed. Here was a pathway to healing and spiritual recovery.

The Quilt finds a home

In 2015 the Quilt was accepted into the permanent collection of the Museum of Australian Democracy at Eureka (MADE), Ballarat where it was on permanent display for almost 3 years. The wall card displayed next to the Quilt read:

MADE recognises the importance and power of the Quilt as a grassroots democratic symbol in light of the historical ongoing inquest into the issues it addresses, and the potential for its messages to reach huge audiences by engaging artists to collaborate with the creators.

Following closure of MADE in 2018, the Museum of Australian Democracy (MoAD) at Old Parliament House in Canberra accepted the Quilt as part of their permanent collection where it now resides.

The Quilt was last displayed in King's Hall at Old Parliament House, Canberra to mark the National Apology to Victims of Institutional Child Sexual Abuse delivered by the Prime Minister Scott Morrison on 22nd October 2018. The following was noted in an article published at the time

MoAD recognises the importance of the Quilt, stitched with messages of resilience and survival, as a symbol of democratic activism in light of the Royal Commission and the apology to victims[9]

The National Quilt Register describes the Quilt as a "living memorial for victims of sexual abuse" and suggests that 'art has the power to heal great atrocities, educate new generations about impact and avoidance and act as memorials for those who suffered … art is the conduit".

Indeed, the Quilt is a conduit to heal, educate, and serves as an enduring memorial. It was created at a time when the avalanche of revelations regarding the atrocities committed by the Catholic Church began. With the passage of time and continued exposure of decades of crime committed by the Church since its' creation, the Quilt now serves as an important tangible artefact that contributes to the narrative of the social history of clerical child sexual abuse in the Ballarat Diocese. The stories behind the blocks are in essence the stories of many.

Endnotes

1. Gero, A. (2008). *The Fabric of Society: Australia's quilt heritage from convict times to 1960.* Australia: The Beagle Press. (p10).
2. Hunter, C. (2019). *Threads of Life,* (2019). Australia: Harry N Abrams, (p276).
3. Gero, A. (2008). *The Fabric of Society: Australia's quilt heritage from convict times to 1960.* Australia: The Beagle Press. (p9).
4. Moving Towards Justice. (2015). *Submission to the Royal Commission on Institutional Responses to Child Sexual Abuse.* Australia: Australian Government. (2015). Retrieved from http://www/childabuseroyalcommission.gov.au
5. https://www.aidsmemorial.org/quilt-history
6. Snibson, L. (2016). *Moving Towards Justice: A local public response to the revelation of historical clerical sexual abuse in the Diocese of Ballarat.* [Unpublished] (p22)
7. Ibid (p24)
8. O'Connor, H. (2013). *The Challenge of Change: Mercy and Loreto Sisters in Ballarat 1950 – 1980.* Ballan, Victoria: Connor Court Publishing Pty Ltd
9. Musa, H. (2018, October 22). *Quilt recognises suffering of abuse victims.* Canberra City News. Retrieved from http://www.citynews.com.au

PART B

Stories of Hope and Despair

Chapter 4

The Burden of Unbearable Knowledge

Carmel Moloney and Margot Serch

"We will not be turned around, or interrupted by intimidation, because we know our inaction and inertia will be the inheritance of the next generation. Our blunders become their burdens."[1]
Anna Gorman

As one of the founding members of the group, Moving Towards Justice (MTJ), Carmel Moloney (nee Bell) played a central role in the creation of the Quilt of Hope. For as long as I can remember,

Carmel was always engaged in community activities and worked to address social injustice wherever she could.

Born the eldest daughter of two in 1938 in Ballarat, Victoria, Carmel attended Mary's Mount Kindergarten, Pleasant Street State School and Ballarat High School to complete her high school certificate. Raised in the Anglican faith, Carmel lived during a time of religious division between Catholics and Protestants and writes of her experience,

> *From a quiet home and small beginnings in a small country town my first memories of my childhood was knowing I lived in a safe loving home. Our street was close to St Patrick's College and Ballarat College, a Presbyterian Faith boys' college.*
>
> *The families on our street consisted of five Catholic families and five families from different denominations. We were Church of England – Anglican. There was a Methodist, a Baptist and a Presbyterian. Also a Salvation Army family lived on the opposite side of the street.*
>
> *The only time I was aware of our different faith and culture was when the children gathered outside our homes to play cricket on the street, we would be interrupted by the Catholics being called in to say the Rosary. There was no other disharmony. It was a given that we went to different Churches and schools. As an Anglican, I would go to Sunday School and to a Eucharist Service similar to a Catholic Mass.*
>
> *Following high school, I worked as a dental nurse before commencing training at Ballarat Base Hospital in 1956, graduating as a State Registered Nurse in 1960. Father Patrick Downes was the Chaplain at this public hospital. Father Downes was a generous, caring, friendly priest, and I was influenced by his kindness. So when he became aware I was seeing a Catholic boy, Frank Moloney, he became interested in my intentions and eventually suggesting that he was available to discuss what was involved in a 'mixed marriage'. So began my weekly visits and instruction in the Catholic faith.*

In the early years as a convert there was great hope and optimism. In the Ballarat Diocese there was a vibrant group of Catholic laity who emerged from the Young Catholic Workers (YCW) mentored by priests who had been chaplains' in the YCW. Influenced by Cardinal Cardijn, a Belgium priest and founder of the YCW, his methodology of "see, judge and act" was encouraging social activism and social justice, encouraging lay people to have a more inclusive role in the Church and a greater awareness of social issues and justice in their communities. Ecumenism was realised when men and women from other faiths formed Action for World Development (AWD). It was an ecumenical program jointly sponsored by the Australian Council of Churches representing Anglican and Protestant denominations and the Australian Epitopal Conference representing the Catholic Church. The challenge was to link the Christian faith with social and political change and addressing world poverty. AWD overrode differences and their friendships remain strong to this day.

My early years as a convert coincided with Vatican II in the 1960s when Pope John XXIII opened the way for a lay ministry with so much ecumenical goodwill and promoting worldwide Christian unity. There was great hope and optimism for the future of our Church.

My memory is influenced by my lived experience as a midwife at St John of God Hospital for six years. This was a rigid dogmatic belief system that exaggerated guilt about any sexuality. Women enduring sex without love, birthing children they did not choose to have and their bodies exhausted and unprepared only just emerging from childhood themselves. Feeling guilt for the wrong reason. Then becoming aware of the criminal negligent care of their children by misogynistic men indoctrinated into a rule book mentality assuming a competence they did not have. Throughout the 19th and 20th Centuries, and possibly forever, women and children have been victims of sexual depravity venereal disease, aids, syphilis.

Catholic dogma and man-made rules denied women and children protective health cover. Betrayed by the Church they loved, there is a lasting rupture of trust between people that once loved one another.

Child abuse manifested when a failure of leadership caused by hypocritical fear of creating a scandal left many victims confused and alienated.

Social questions in the Catholic Church were a new and unchartered area and Christian Democracy was seen as a dangerous innovation.

We felt the disappointment after Vatican II when the priests we admired left the church and married! Father John Molony was the first priest to leave and marry from our parish that we were aware of. The laity, especially members of the Adult Lay Apostolate as we were known, were saddened to lose John. We respected his decision remaining friends until his death in 2018.

For me, when the Ballarat Red Cross suggested we form a Red Cross unit in Black Hill, I saw it as an opportunity to experience the lay ministry we had hoped for in post-Vatican II and welcomed the opportunity to become a founding member. We were all newlyweds living ordinary lives, raising children, and attending different religious denominations. It could not have been more ecumenical – many faiths meeting in the local Baptist Church Hall and having fundraising events in the Presbyterian and Anglican Church Sunday School halls and breaking bread with women from many different faiths. Our unit in Black Hill survived for over 30 years with only age causing us to retire but with lifelong friendships made.

The Red Cross and Red Crescent represents a worldwide organisation and has operated for over 150 years working to improve the lives of vulnerable people. Promoting humanitarian laws and values, it is not constrained by political, religious, or cultural affiliations. My active membership in our local unit for over 25 years provided an outlet to practise more of the teachings of Jesus that I felt I could not do within the confines of the patriarchal structures of the Catholic Church. I had found my tribe.

In 2011, Carmel's life was transformed in ways she would never have imagined. Margot Serch, a life-long friend, told Carmel that she had been informed by Detective Sergeant Kevin Carson that her only son Michael had been sexually abused when he was 11 years old by Brother Robert Best at St Leos College, Box Hill. Best had been under investigation and through the evidence gathering process, Michael's name had arisen as a potential victim. Michael subsequently disclosed to Detective Sergeant Kevin Carson that he had been sexually abused by Best after holding the secret for over 35 years.

Row 5 Block 36
Made by Liz Bailey on behalf of Carmel Moloney

Row 3 Block 20
Written by Carmel Moloney, made by Beryl Andersen

Margot's own life had been one of service to others. Her formal training as a nurse had brought her into contact with the homeless and to those with drug and alcohol addictions. Over many years she volunteered much of her time to this group of people. In 2018, she was awarded the Volunteer of the Year award for Eastern Health, which covers public hospitals from Richmond to Healesville.

For Margot, the revelation that her son had been sexually abused by a Christian brother whom she had welcomed into her home for many years was beyond belief. How could this be? This can't be true! How did she not know? The revelation provided an understanding of her son Michael's lifelong struggles and challenges with daily life. Margot writes:

He has had a very difficult life, no friends! Doctors and social workers and case managers make up his day. He is on very heavy medication and a general fear of the world around him. He no longer has the ability to solve problems so relies on us for day-to-day problem-solving assistance.

Brother Best came to my home on occasions and used my trust to abuse my son. I was a single mother at the time.

On two occasions, Michael has attempted suicide.

We attended the court case of Brother Best at the time with my son Michael. He was unable to give evidence as he has a severe mental illness and his psychiatrist thought that it would be too much for him. At an earlier time, he had given a full statement to the solicitor and police.

Carmel and Margot met in kindergarten over 75 years ago and growing up they went to different schools and were part of a different social class and faith. Despite this, they overrode these social differences, and their friendship has remained strong to this day. Carmel writes:

At age 4, my mother enrolled me in a kindergarten at Mary's Mount Sturt Street. A Loreto nun Mother Brendan initiated the idea of a kindergarten that would welcome children from other faiths. Two non-Catholics enrolled, John Shaw a Presbyterian and myself Church of England.

My mother could never imagine the long-term consequences of her decision – 70 years later it was pivotal in the most important insights and life changing decisions I have ever made. From completely different backgrounds and cultures, two 4-year-old girls forged a lifelong friendship.

Margot continued her education at Mary's Mount. I was educated in the state schools primary and Ballarat West High School. This did not stop our paths from crossing, and we kept finding our way back to each other. We shared the love of competitive swimming and belonged to the Midlands Swimming Club. We both chose nursing as a career, Margot trained at St Vincent's Melbourne, and I trained at the Ballarat Base Hospital. After we graduated, we worked together at St John of Gods Hospital in Ballarat.

Married the same year in 1960, as two couples we shared a social life. We never lost touch. Margot has always been my loyal, beautiful childhood friend.

When Margot shared the news of her son's abuse, Carmel was horrified, and her heart went out to her friend as she processed this appalling and confronting information. Here was yet another story she was hearing but this time it was first-hand from someone close to her. Given this truth, was there truth to the stories and innuendos she had heard in hushed conversations over the preceding years? Whilst sporadic revelations of clerical child sexual abuse had emerged in the public realm, the Church had provided reassurance that the cases were few and far between and that victims were being supported through channels such as Towards Healing and the Melbourne Response. Was the problem more widespread than the abnormal behaviour of the few such as Ridsdale – the case they had known about when he was first convicted in 1994?

We were so removed from it. Half of us did not even know what abuse was. We heard "this priest has a problem". I think when he (Ridsdale) was first charged, we were told he had been sent to America and that Bishop Mulkearns believed that he had been cured... It is a church that has not allowed people to think for themselves a lot. We have believed everything they have told us. We have trusted them[2].

Sharing Margot's story with other members of the St Columbus Bereavement team, they all 'began to really listen, to ask questions of Church leaders and communities, and to read widely'[3].

As they engaged with the topic to learn more, it was emerging that the story of Margot and her son Michael was one of many. It was becoming apparent that clerical child sexual abuse within their Church was an epidemic rather than confined to isolated cases. What began as providing support to a friend and her family transformed into the forming of a small group that became Moving Towards Justice (MTJ). Carmel writes,

> *Margot's story coincided with my being invited to join the St Columbus Bereavement team. While I was still attending mass weekly, the only contribution I made to Parish life was being on the floral roster. I joined the Bereavement team because of my relationship with Maree Phelan.*
>
> *The timing and my willingness to re-engage with Church life was with a new awareness manifesting through what amounted to insights and revelations.*

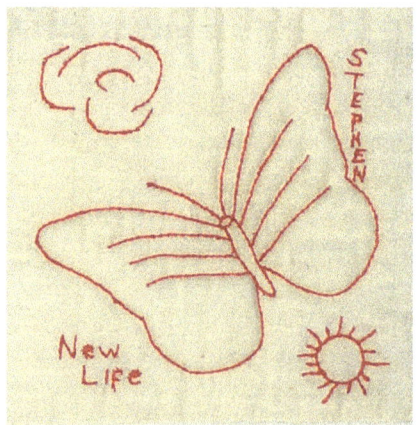
Row 4 Block 32
Anonymous maker (mother)

Row 8 Block 60
Anonymous maker (mother)

One such revelation was learning the reason behind why a mother who had been a dedicated parishioner left the Church to join the Church of Christ congregation. This faith was so far removed from

Catholicism, we referred to them as "born again Christians". Given her religious commitment to the Church, this came as a surprise to me, and I wondered what had made her leave. When I asked another parishioner, they told me she had left as her two boys had been sexually abused and she wasn't getting any support from the Church. She had experienced the same deafening silence from the Church and parishioners as I was to learn from so many others. This was in my parish, why didn't we know?

I contacted an old friend, Evelyn, who attended the same Church of Christ congregation. We had remained friends having trained at Ballarat Base Hospital and catching up at reunions. Over coffee she not only confirmed what I had been told about the woman leaving our parish but also imparted several other stories she knew of victims and their families. We were two women sharing stories of mothers with disbelief and dismay. Supporting our early efforts, Evelyn attended our meetings and Kitchen Table Spirituality, reaching out to mothers of abused children and introducing us to likeminded members of the Church of Christ and Uniting Care. During this time our religious differences were so insignificant, our ideas of how to support victims similar.

As our group learnt more, we struggled with what to do with the topic that was discussed openly and protecting the Church was paramount. Silence was the preferred option to avoid facing a truth they didn't want to believe. We were more shocked that Catholic women didn't want to talk about it or acknowledge it. The silence of good people who do nothing!

I approached Sister Rita Hayes to talk about it as I knew she had connections with Margot's family. The Sisters of Mercy immediately offered support and opened their home for meetings to be held.

There were many key people in the formation of MTJ. One of the most important conduits I made was with Rosalie Sheehan, wife of Frank Sheehan (RIP 2021) who became the intrepid leader of MTJ. Under his leadership we never looked back. It was as if his life's journey from YCW Action for World Development, the Adult Lay Apostolate, and as a politician in the Caine Labour Government crossing swords with Pell and Santamaria prepared him for the final contribution, challenging the Church he loved and remained loyal to.

As a founding member of MTJ, Carmel did what she does best and connected people, providing safe emotional space for stories to be heard and believed. She openly challenged the narrative of the Church and spoke her mind to priests she had known and respected for many years. Carmel was relentless in sharing information and key publications to raise awareness of the impact of the past atrocities. Voicing her views, she found to her dismay, there were friends she was not able to speak to about it as they were not prepared to listen or friends that avoided the topic as they knew Carmel's position on it.

As the depth of depravity continued to be revealed, Carmel felt the guilt of living such a joyous life whilst simultaneously there had been so much evil going on within the Church, in her community. The guilt of blissful ignorance and blind faith prevented her from knowing, hearing, and questioning earlier whispers of "Father behaving inappropriately" and what that meant. She felt betrayed by the institution and hierarchy of the Church, the community of parishioners and by her own faith. Acting with courage and conviction, Carmel undertook whatever action she could within her power to support those that had suffered such immense injustice.

In December 2012, Carmel provided a powerful submission to the Family and Community Development Committee's *Inquiry into Handling of Child Abuse by Religious and Other Non-Government Organisations.*

During the past twelve months I have completed my second conversion, one from illusion to reality. It has been more painful than my conversion from Anglicanism to Catholicism more than 50 years ago when I embraced the Catholic church, its theology and the many dedicated priests, religious and laity I found within its community.

The Burden of Unbearable Knowledge

I recently re-read an article by Professor Caroline Taylor in a July 2002 edition of the Ballarat Courier. A decade on, nothing has changed. There is still a medieval mindset by the Church hierarchy. Professor Taylor commented on a USA Bishop's Conference where several Bishops showed leadership, condemning the failure of the Church hierarchy to act proactively and decisively against child abuse by members of the clergy. This failure is intended to maintain the status and the authority of the Church, and ignores the suffering of innocent children, victimised by predatory priests and religious. They care more about protecting the church than the victims.

Row 9 Block 67
Unknown Maker

Row 8 Block 63
Unknown Maker

Some clergy and laity appear angry and confused about the current media scrutiny. Some of this is understandable, particularly when it appears to imply guilt by association for the current clergy and community. Some laity and religious continue this victim-blaming and are angry that the church has been brought into disrepute. The history of inaction by the bishops helps no-one. The reaction of some of the laity is cynical, especially about the issue of compensation; as if compensation could suddenly cure the pain of the victims; surely compensation is a recognition of their suffering, acknowledging nothing can restore the childhood.

Nothing can erase the horror of the serious forms of abuse and rape by evil men and the guilt they imposed on these innocent children who carried that guilt forward into manhood, despite their innocence. The secondary victims are the parents and siblings, whose sacrifice, loving care and nurturing has been trashed by the vanity of men who instituted fear and self-loathing that silenced these innocent children for years. When they finally found the courage to speak, they were betrayed and maligned again.

So many children have carried this evil in their psyche, trapped in their childhood, living with self-loathing, anxiety, and resentment, with little or no sense of purpose. They are certainly not the 'Beloved' of the church community. That community needs to answer the question St Jerome posed: if the truth offends you, it is better to be offended than the truth be concealed. Has the Catholic Church betrayed its own humanity? The lay community has the right to question why the most vulnerable and least powerful have been wronged and sadly maligned by men who claim they have the mandate to proclaim the healing message of Christianity but who are indifferent to argument and compassion.

Is the reality that ten years after Professor Taylor urged a more compassionate response to clerical abuse that nothing has changed, that women, children and gays have no placed in the Catholic community?

As one of the survivors of clerical abuse urged: "Please do not let us suffer in vain. There must be a reason for our suffering."

It's the sadness of betrayal and trust between people that once loved each other.

Throughout the public hearings, Carmel and other MTJ members travelled the hour and half train journey to Melbourne on multiple occasions to bear witness to the inquiry hearings. It was during these journeys that they heard the personal stories of victims and their families first-hand as they too travelled for the hearings. What was revealed to her was beyond belief and provided further impetus for Carmel to do what she could to help those impacted by the actions of the Church and to agitate for change.

A month after the public hearings had commenced for the Victorian Inquiry in October 2012, the then Prime Minister Julia Gillard announced the decision to establish the *Royal Commission into Institutional Responses to Child Sexual Abuse*. I remember the day Carmel rang me to share the news of the announcement. She was exuberant as it provided further validation that there was a truth to be uncovered and the voices that had been silenced for decades would be heard and believed. A form of justice could be achieved.

The following year on 13th November 2013, Carmel and other MTJ members stood on the steps of Parliament in Melbourne along with others at the Rally of Hope Celebration for the release of the Victorian Inquiry's final report, *Betrayal of Trust*. It was an emotional moment. During this moment, Carmel and Lyn Snibson held up the unfinished Quilt of Hope with a small selection of blocks in their hands. One of the blocks displayed the name Mick Serch (Margot's son) and it was fortuitous that he was there that day. His block was one of the first to be requested by Carmel.

> *When I spoke to Michael and asked what he would like on his block for the Quilt, he simply said, "Just Mick Serch". It was an opportunity to record his name publicly as he had not been able to give evidence in the court case of Brother Best.*
>
> *Michael was able to attend the Rally, thanks to his case worker. He appeared on the steps of Parliament and joined us as we unfurled The Quilt of Hope – unfinished but Michael's block "Mick Serch" was front and centre. He was warmly received as we embraced him. The Press became aware and interested. They were gentle and kind and Michael was humble and polite with his answers. This was a time that had been a long time coming. Michael was able to redefine*

himself – he DID matter, his story was important. Love energised him. Without his courage and Margot's love, there would never have been a Quilt of Hope or a book.

For Carmel, it was a special moment to stand with Michael (aka Mick) knowing the courage and determination it had taken for him to attend the event.

The release of 'Betrayal of Trust' that named communities across the Ballarat Diocese reverberated throughout the community. What followed in subsequent years was a tsunami of revelations that added to the weight of what Carmel refers to as "the burden of unbearable knowledge".

Attending in person to witness the Royal Commission hearings in Ballarat, an uglier and more sinister truth was revealed of not only the extent of clerical child sexual abuse, but also the far-reaching active cover up undertaken by the Catholic Church over decades. The only saving grace was that it was now being revealed on a national stage with the findings released in December 2017.

It has been a tumultuous decade, during which time Carmel ceaselessly supported those impacted by clerical child sexual abuse and advocated for their voices to be heard. The rage still exists as does the ongoing disgust in a Church that has continued to fail to support victims and their families. When thinking of Margot and knowing the challenges she has faced, Carmel is appalled that someone who has dedicated so much of her life for those less fortunate was not given any acknowledgement or support from the Church or parishioners in her time of need.

After a lifetime of giving selflessly, when her time came, no-one stepped forward to offer support or care…inertia and denial…it disgusts me that to this day, no-one in that parish or the Church has ever offered her support. Again, it is the deafening silence of good people that choose to do nothing.

Margot has been stoic in overcoming many challenges and surviving the lifelong heartache of witnessing that her son was unable to live a life of joy and happiness – a life without peace. She is like gold in the fire. Instead of destroying her, this suffering has alchemised into compassion and empathy for those in the community who are marginalised and powerless.

Reflecting on what has come to pass, Carmel feels relief as she has been "freed up to have an autonomous conscience". She has relinquished the obligation to an outdated doctrine and a Church that actively covered up crimes committed against children.

Looking back over the past 10 years, seeing what is true and clear in this moment and experiencing what physical reality comes with awareness opens the door to true freedom. No longer acting outside integrity or conforming to a belief system inherited from a tribe, parents, role models and friends. Being able to honour values and convictions to live in alignment with them to put you on the path to fulfilling your life's purpose.

Carmel is now able to sit with some peace that from the moment of her awakening in 2011, she did what she could for others and stood by her convictions to walk away from the Church. The Quilt of Hope (and this book) provide a lasting testament to the inspired action taken by Carmel and a group of like-minded people.

Afterthought

Looking back, Carmel is aware that as the sixties were drawing to a close, women were facing the reality that there would be no respite, just more of the same. By the 1970s however, women began to experience for the first time, a reform agenda that would involve them at the highest level of government and in a society in which women and men of Australia would be equals.

The Whitlam government 1972-1975 was the first national government to implement a big reform agenda for women. Those changes amounted to a social and economic revolution for women. They formed movements that empowered them to effect change in community attitudes. Their involvement in the anti-Vietnam movement exposed women for the first time to radical action.

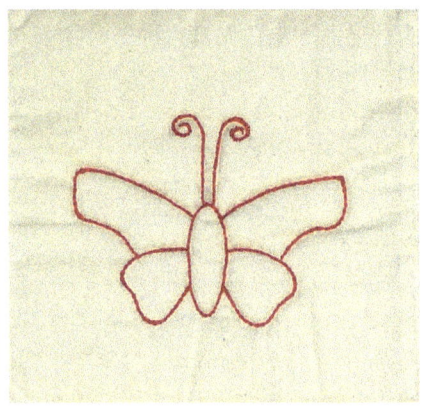

Row 2 Block 12
Unknown

Row 9 Block 72
Anonymous

During this time, the collective trauma of child abuse shifted the cultural identity of the laity as Catholics and the quality of communal life diminished. The acceptance of uncomfortable truths challenged their loyalty to the Catholic Church. Many will never recover or forget and as adults will only give loyalty if they are listened to and respected as adults.

Endnotes

1   Gorman, A. (2021). *The Hill We Climb: An inaugural poem.* Chatto and Windus, pg. 23
2   (Vic Inquiry Transcript, Dec 2010)
3   (MTJ Doc pg 12).

Chapter 5

The Ripple Effects
(*name changed to preserve anonymity)

In 2013, Carmel Moloney invited Diane* to do a block for the Quilt after they met at a gathering in Ballarat. The square she embroidered is a house with a path leading up to it. Diane's square is the "hope of a happy ending". Growing up, she dreamed of being married and raising children in a happy home.

It has been a long, arduous, and heartbreaking journey for Diane and her family over the past 40 years. She has carried the burden of knowledge that her two boys (now in their 40's) were sexually abused in primary school by parish priest Gerald Ridsdale. He was a priest who had disguised himself as a family friend, confidant and who had joined in many family occasions. Diane has held the weight of regret, silence, disbelief, and shame. She has had to fight for justice, fight to be heard, and importantly fight for her boys' right to be understood.

When asked to contribute to this book, Diane was extremely hesitant. For so many years she has told her story and not been believed or listened to.

Diane has endured the emotional pain of the weight of others' inaction despite the painful retelling of her story – the story of her boys, the story of what it has meant for her family, the dreams for her children who as a mother she watched being ravaged.

But it is also Diane's story of reliance and tenacity and a mother's love for her children that grows stronger in adversity. She wanted to write her story knowing that it is important and needs to be heard. In a card sent with a handwritten draft chapter, Diane wrote "I do think it has given me some peace to write things down; there are many stories entwined with others over many years - too many stories most sad" (card dated 25/2/19).

Demonstrating her commitment for the story to be told, Diane provided me with three drafts, all 8 pages handwritten to tell her story in her words, her voice. It has been a privilege to be trusted by Diane to collaborate with her to write it. It is her story and no-one else can write it better than her.

The chapter that follows comes from the handwritten drafts provided by Diane along with diary entries, letters and other documents approved by her for use in the Chapter. These sources span the period between 1994 and 2019.

***

"Our journey in life leads in many different ways, this is mine."
Diane

In 1994 one Saturday morning, while having breakfast with our daughter at a Melbourne street café, I saw the headlines "Gerald Ridsdale convicted and sentenced to 15 years in jail for sexual abuse to children".

I froze. I knew then that life for us as a family was going to be shaken to its core. A mother's deepest horror, my two boys had attended school where Father Gerald Ridsdale was the Parish Priest. At that moment I knew this was the reason for the downward descent of our boys. I knew our nightmare was going to continue. The boys were already spiralling out of control, and we could not understand why. Seeing the headlines and reading the article, my heart sank. I felt a sudden dread at the realisation that our boys had been sexually abused by Ridsdale.

Row 5 Block 38, Diane and John

Row 5 Block 40 Unknown Maker

On our way home we spoke about asking the boys and getting help. We asked one son and he denied it again and again. Our other son said, "No but I think my brother was and we should try to help him before he commits suicide". For eight years, they constantly denied the abuse. Then at Easter time in 2002, our son, who was now in his late 20's, broke down and cried in his father's arms. We suffered as a family, the early smoking, the early alcohol abuse, reckless behaviour, no respect for authority, the fights, and quarrels late at night after a family get together and too much alcohol, the enormous financial and emotional impact.

I did think some person from the church would knock on our door and offer help as the boys had been altar boys when Ridsdale was parish priest. But that never happened. I think I thought that someone would knock on our door because I saw that as their duty of care. Would the church not want to openly reach out to children and families who had been in contact with Ridsdale? Would they not for their own peace of mind and for their own ethos of care for others want to check and want to know? It became clear to me that they (the Church) did not want to know; they did not want to take responsibility; they wanted to remain silent, and they wanted us to remain silent. Their self-righteousness continues to this day.

As a young girl, my ambition was not to travel the world but to be married, have children, and live happily ever after. The dream started when I met a handsome young farmer and married. Children came along. We lived on a farm and the children were very happy spending time with their dad. Riding horses, droving cattle, doing sheep work, and being there at shearing time was always a lot of fun. Playing in the creek at the bottom of the house was always a favourite past time that the two boys enjoyed with their sister tagging along.

Our son was to start school so we sent him to the local state school. When he was getting to the age of 1st communion and our other son was to start school and as I was Catholic, we looked at sending them to a Catholic school. So, then our three children started at a Catholic school, where Fr Gerald Ridsdale was parish priest.

As time went by the boys became enemies, not fighting as such, but not friends any more. Our sons changed, and I don't know how but my husband and I would often go to bed and wonder what we were doing wrong. I would talk to my mum about how the boys had changed from happy friends to adversaries.

Our sons struggled all the time at school and didn't seem to learn. The teachers did all they could and so did I, but nothing worked. They were getting worse and when they had the opportunity to move school, my husband and I wondered why they were so keen to move. It was only later as time went on, we understood why. We had meeting after meeting with teachers as school was a continuous struggle for them. They left school early.

Both boys became dependent on alcohol and cigarettes at an early age. As a mother I looked at other families and wondered why mine was so different. The happy family circle was just not there. We had lots of family time together, but you were very aware of the tension and the waiting for the next argument to start. I would go to bed relieved and thankful when we had a happy night and hoping the next family get together will be just as good.

As a mother I struggled to keep the family together. We wondered why the boys were slowly self-destructing after they left school. Our daughter was a happy girl who worked hard at school and also went to the Catholic college. She completed Year 12 and went on to Uni, where she worked hard to achieve success. My husband and I wondered why she was able to work at school and achieve what she set out to do, while the boys with the same parents were unable to settle and learn at school.

***

Another argument between the boys late on Saturday night in October 1999 was very violent. Ridsdale's name kept coming into the argument. The eldest disappeared into the night and we didn't see him until the next day. It was very upsetting – the not knowing.

Sometime later, I spoke to a lady who had a lot to do with the church and told her of my fear of the boys being abused. I told her about the fights, the drinking, all the unhappy times and how we were looking for some kind of help or guidance as the boys were slowly self-destructing. She was very understanding as she knew about Ridsdale as her sister, a teacher, was at the Mortlake School when Ridsdale was removed.

My days were full of sadness and torment. The next day she gave me a pamphlet for Towards Healing (Hurt or Distressed?) and she said you can get a pamphlet from the back of the church. The church is the last place a victim wants to go to. Years later I asked Bishop Connors to put the pamphlet in sports clubs or hotels where victims might find them and get help. But no, nothing was done. The pamphlet can still be found at the back of the church.

I also made many phone calls to other parishioners, but no-one wanted to know. It was often a wall of silence trying to get to the truth. Sometimes when I made a phone call, I would be told to never ring again, and they would hang up. I met with a nun who had been a teacher at the same school my children attended at the time Ridsdale was the parish priest and the boys were altar boys. We sat and spoke about Ridsdale. He was in jail for 15 years for abuse of children at the school she had been teaching at.

As we chatted, she showed no emotion when I expressed my concern about my boys being abused. Her only comment was "no, your boys were too young". She thought this was the case as the sentence he was serving was for abuse on older children. I thought, "great, our boys are safe," but as time went on, we knew they had been abused. I later learnt that Mercy Nuns had been ordered by Bishop Mulkearns not to discuss Ridsdale.

After reading the pamphlet, I rang 'Towards Healing' and spoke to Shane Wall. I was very upset at the time and stated the boys were altar boys to Ridsdale and we needed help or some guidance to save the boys from destroying themselves and their family. I wanted help as the mother of boys I suspected had been abused. I wanted to know where to get help and what to do about it if the boys told us. I was told there was no help for families or parents of children who suspected abuse. If the boys wanted help, they could ring Towards Healing between 9am-4pm and leave a message and they would get back to them. The boys had to come forward for there to be help for them.

This phone call upset me more as I had sent my children to a Catholic school where the duty of care had been broken. Ridsdale had been sentenced in 1994 to 15 years jail for abuse in the 1970s. The church was doing nothing for the family; the only help they would give was to the boys, not the family, and only if the boys came forward.

They did not want to know about the pain and the struggle that our family was having and the torment our boys were suffering in silence. I rang again and stated how hard it was on our family to know that our boys had been abused to some degree and what can I do, where can I get help? I was told again there was no help until the boys came forward. Where was the compassion? Where was the sense of care? Wouldn't they want to know? Wouldn't they want to reach out for their own peace of mind, for their own duty of care to help find the truth of what may have occurred to my boys and many others?

All my reading of sexual abuse and disclosures of sexual abuse is about extending the support, being there and being open. Why would they not want to help to understand the truth as to why my boys were in pain? They knew more than we did and knew about Ridsdale. I think sadly, that is why they did not want to seek any more truths. Years passed, as did the continuous pain at watching the boys slowly self-destruct.

Then at Easter time 2002, our son cried in his father's arms as he told him he had been abused by Ridsdale when at primary school. The Hurt and Distressed pamphlet has always been by our phone hoping the boys would see it and ring and get help.

I rang 'Towards Healing' on Friday and Saturday morning in a distressed state and told them our son had revealed he had been abused by Ridsdale when he was in primary school. It wasn't until Monday morning Allan Spencer rang back. Allan was a voice on the phone working with 'Towards Healing'. His understanding of the pain the family had and the shame, guilt, confusion, and struggle

The Story of the Quilt of Hope

the victims suffer was outstanding. I had a lot of phone calls to and from Allan. Bill Radly, a counsellor, is also a man who understood the victim's struggles. Each man gave our son their after-hours number; this was used many times.

On one occasion Allan received a phone call at 4am and he was able to calm the situation. Allan rang us early the next morning and we removed all guns from the farm (guns are used on the farm for injured animals or vermin). The alarming reality of the level of distress and pain our son was in was heart-wrenching. Both men gave our son some hope and help to build strength to keep going when alcohol and depression were taking over. Our other son refused counselling and to this day has had none. Our struggle to keep the boys safe and maintain some form of life continued. Many a time if the phone rang late at night, we would answer waiting to hear some bad news, it never came. The constant thought of suicide was always with us.

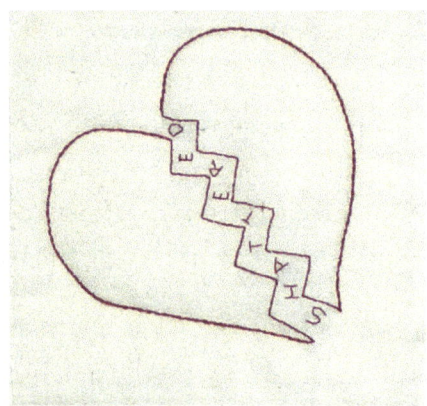

Row 8 Block 62
Unknown

Row 6 Block 41
Maker Unknown

'Towards Healing' only took phone calls from 9-4 Monday to Friday or you could ring and leave a message. Most victims need help between 9pm – 6am and weekends. These young men are suffering with their day-to-day tasks - thinking of suicide, overdose, their next drink, broken families, trying to hold down a job. They cannot wait for 'Towards Healing' to ring back and in some cases, victims receive no help and struggle on the best they can.

At one of the many meetings we had with Bishop Connors, I asked him to consider changing the hours of Towards Healing so victims could ring late at night and at weekends when they were often at their lowest. Nothing was done. The problem still exists, the Church with all of its wealth and pageantry still does not understand the needs of parishioners and their families.

***

In 2002, Diane's son completed a police statement with Detective Sergeant Kevin Carson. He had been investigating new allegations against Ridsdale (and Robert Best) since 2001 and was working with other victims on their statements and evidence to ascertain whether a potential further prosecution would occur. The burden of proof lay with the victims.

***

I wrote to Cardinal Pell (Archbishop of Sydney at the time) in October 2002. His response gave me no hope. The Catholic Church claims to understand the effects sexual abuse has on young victims and their families. But do they? Cardinal Pell did say he would "pray for me," but offered no guidance even though he had set up the 'Melbourne Response' in 1996. A cap of $50,000 would silence victims and the problem would go away. The problem continues. The Church still lacks or chooses to ignore the deep understanding of the effect sexual abuse has on victims and families.

Shane Wall stated at the start of our first meeting with 'Towards Healing', that "$1million wouldn't be enough compensation for all the pain and suffering. The church does not deny your abuse as we have read the police report." I had many phone calls with Shane Wall who I found was very difficult to deal with as was Bishop

Peter Connors. Their lack of empathy and understanding of sexual abuse was unconscionable. As time went on, the Bishop seemed to begin to understand the heartache I was suffering and on occasions showed some level of compassion.

Diary entry, 1 Feb 2003

A very difficult day today. I was surprised by Shane Wall's attitude when John and I arrived with our son and lawyer. The Bishop also showed hostility. Shane Wall did apologise to our son saying, "One million dollars wouldn't be enough compensation for the pain and suffering and the Church does not deny the abuse as they have read the police report, but also $200,000 was unreasonable and that wouldn't happen".

Our lawyer made comment about events that took place around the time of our sons' abuse. The Bishop said, "That was 20 years ago and I am not going over and over that again." I was so disappointed in this comment as the Church failed in its duty of care to me as a young Catholic mother and my two innocent boys over 25 years ago and that pain and suffering still continues today. Bishop Peter Connors apologized to our son.

As we were driving home that day, our son made comment that the Bishop made a very poor apology. It was just another thing he had to do that day. Our son said at mediation he wanted continuous counselling for all members of his family and payment for the secondary education of his children. Our son asked the Bishop did he think this was unreasonable and the Bishop said "No Comment!" John then said there would also be monetary compensation. The Bishop said the Church has paid up to $55,000.

How dare they put all victims in the same basket depending on what and how many times those young boys were violated.

As time went on the church itself demanded three psychiatric reports. That in itself was distressing for the boys to have to continue to relive the nightmare of their childhood. Reading those reports was heart wrenching and we realised the enormity of the trauma our sons were suffering and how dysfunctional they had become. We understood how life has become for them, the dread of the next day.

The church expects victims to come forward to get help or sort themselves out. The church doesn't understand. Many victims haven't got the finances, ability, or strength to take action. Unless you have strength and perseverance the church will not listen to you. The church failed in their duty of care to our boys and many other victims and their families. As many victims don't come forward the church thinks this is a small problem.

The memories keep coming back. At that time, we were going through Australia's worst drought, interest rates were 24% on our overdraft, sheep had to be shot, and income on the land was at an all-time low. We struggled through each day - my husband working hard on and off the land to make ends meet as I continued to maintain the daily chores of life. I was constantly thinking of what had to be done to help our family. This situation placed enormous strain on our relationship emotionally and on our intimacy. At times, alcohol was used as a comfort for my husband, and I slipped into depression. We worked hard to maintain our relationship with each other and our children. I had feelings of guilt about my commitment to the Catholic faith and my naivety in blindly respecting the status and authority of the Church then feeling the loss of faith, a faith that had been my heritage and a big part of my life was overwhelming.

We had the support of Detective Sergeant Kevin Carson while we got proof the boys were altar boys to Ridsdale and they went to the same parish school when Ridsdale was parish priest. Ridsdale had always offered to help. He was there on school sports days, school excursions and many other activities. He was parish priest for their First Communion and Confirmation. I went to the local town and got the newspapers out of the archives looking for confirmation on dates of town events the parish school attended, finding old class school photos and photos of First Communion and Confirmation. We had to have proof of all occasions for compensation with Towards Healing and it was necessary for the prosecution of Ridsdale. This was long and tedious.

Diary entry, 22 Feb 2003

All this week I have been working on the 19 requests from our son's lawyer. Looking for class photos and naming the children, looking for school reports and photos and dates of communion and confirmation. The Bishop said that the Church was doing all they can – but are they?! What are they doing for the family? The Church has set up a Professional Standards Resource Group to receive and handle complaints. What about trying to understand the heartache of the parents of the victims? You would think the Bishop would go to the grass roots of his diocese and put in place a support group for families and victims. I know not all families and victims would want to go but even if the Church was able to help one family find peace! They should do everything in their power to do so.

Our son has never told us all of the violations he suffered until this week and the disbelief to learn his first communion and confirmation were two of many occasions was devastating. Ridsdale, this horrendous man, took the innocence from our fun-loving little boys. It has pierced my soul and broken my heart forever.

Our sons' journey in life changed to one of mistrust, continuous struggle, loneliness, and difficulties in many aspects of life. I now hope as our sons have come forward the direction of their life will change, and peace of mind will come. The Church, which failed in its duty of care, will not insult them further with a $50,000 pay out.

***

In October 2003, the brief of evidence was submitted to the then Office of Public Prosecutions (OPP) Director, Paul Coghlan for consideration for a further prosecution of Ridsdale who was currently serving a prison sentence and due for release. Six months later, in April 2004, Detective Sergeant Carson received advice that the OPP would *not authorise the prosecution of Ridsdale. A letter received by Diane and John's son from Detective Sergeant Carson stated that:*

> *...the Court of Criminal Appeal described Ridsdale's sentence as "harsh", "virtual life sentence", "unusually long"" and "harsh punishment and a severe burden". "While sympathising with the complainants it was considered that given the limited sentencing options available, any further prosecution of Ridsdale is not in the public interest".*

It was devastating news for the victims, and they were outraged as to how this decision was made. Diane and John contacted Detective Sergeant Carson to request a meeting with the OPP Director so they could speak directly with him to seek answers as to why the decision had been made. This meeting was arranged and in December 2004, Diane, John, and other victims spoke passionately about the enormity of the impact that the sexual abuse committed upon them by Ridsdale has had, and continues to have, on their lives. Two months later, in February 2005, Detective Sergeant Carson was advised that the brief of evidence was authorized for prosecution. Diane shares her memories of this time and the action she undertook to ensure the prosecution of Ridsdale would not be dismissed.

✻✻✻

Paul Coghlan, Director of Public Prosecutions, stated that it was not in the public interest to prosecute Ridsdale with more charges of sexual abuse against children. Ridsdale was in jail serving a 15-year sentence and about to be released. I made many phone calls to the Office of Public Prosecution and spoke to Anne O'Brien, who was the Senior Social Worker at the OPP trying to understand the decision not to prosecute Ridsdale.

Detective Sergeant Carson arranged a meeting with Mr Coghlan. He was a gentle man and had empathy for us as parents. A very heated debate followed. We pointed out to Mr Coghlan how unfair it was that Ridsdale was being released and our boys and many others would not be heard, or he would not be punished for all his horrendous crimes on them. There are many victims that suffered sexual abuse by Ridsdale as he was being moved from parish to parish by the Catholic Church. The victims are now in their late 20-30s and Mr Coghlan wondered why they had not come forward earlier.

I explained to him that victims cannot come forward on cue. Victims of abuse can't come forward until they're ready, often in their 30s. If the Church and the law had taken the time to study the effect of sexual abuse on young children, they would have understood. I was astonished at their lack of knowledge and understanding of the damage sexual abuse has on the development of children and the lifelong impact it has. It has remained a lingering question for me as to whether they did not know of the dynamics of sexual abuse - or whether they did not want to know - the latter perhaps leading to their inaction at the very personal level and at the cost of the children and families affected.

Detective Sergeant Carson rang us the next week and said, "You've done it, we are going to court". I started to campaign to get as many victims to come forward as the OPP stated that there was a chance Ridsdale would not be prosecuted again. I rang or visited all the Editors of the local papers where Ridsdale had been parish priest, asking them to write an article on Ridsdale and encouraging victims to make contact with Detective Sergeant Carson.

It was a tedious task as Ridsdale had been moved 10 times across Victoria. Parishioners were always surprised to find Ridsdale gone. He was their parish priest and then gone and moved on to another country town at short notice. Moving Ridsdale to the country, Mulkearns stated there was less temptation in the country, hoping the problem would go away. At mediation I asked the question, "Were country children less important than city children? Ridsdale was still being reported to the Bishop for abusing children.

We went to court and Ridsdale was sentenced to another 13 years. The stories we heard that day broke my heart again. Our boys were the only boys that had support by parents. Suicide, overdose, alcohol abuse, broken families and parents not believing their children - many victims were at the court alone that day. The Court Clerk had tears in his eyes and had to stop many times as he read out the charges. I left the court room in the middle of proceedings and wept. To hear the extent of abuse on these young boys was unbearable. We all left court that day emotionally and mentally battered. Detective Sergeant Carson was with us every step of the way. His friendship to us and other victims is lasting. Anne O'Brien was also in court with us on that day.

Row 3 Block 18
Unknown

Row 3 Block 24
Unknown Maker

The boys received compensation after a long battle with the church, but no amount of compensation will replace their childhood and the chance to live a happy life and to achieve their full potential. Early sexual abuse destroys the development in children and unless the church is prepared to understand the full consequence of sexual abuse, the pain and suffering will continue. Financial compensation is not the only answer. The victims were given a life sentence at an early age. They need a lifetime of love, guiding support and understanding. The strength my sons have to continue against adversity is remarkable. My love and respect for them is unending.

The Story of the Quilt of Hope

There have been many sad times throughout our journey – the road has been rough with many bumps along the way. When our daughter got married in a Catholic Church, I didn't realise the effect it would have on the boys and my husband going into the church. It wasn't until afterward that I realized how traumatic it was for them. My husband walked our daughter down the aisle with a look of a ghost; the boys shivered as they watched on. My sister asked afterwards, "What on earth was wrong with them; they all looked so blank."

My husband's parents were outraged by the boy's behaviour, called them a public disgrace, exiling our sons and therefore us. This has been ongoing sadness for my husband. A friend since kindergarten told me we were failures as parents and she no longer wanted to associate with us as the boys were a constant embarrassment to us and the town. I was devastated as our son lay critically injured in hospital as a result of his reckless behaviour. We were rescuing the boys often emotionally, physically, and financially. Their sister doing the best she can to support and have a relationship with her brothers; she is also a secondary victim.

***

Gerald Ridsdale is known as Australia's most notorious paedophile. The destruction he has left throughout Victoria is uncountable. In one court room he stated he thought there would be 100 victims or even more. It saddens me to think Ridsdale's abuse had been reported to Bishop Ronald Mulkearns in the late 1960s, yet as each report came in, Ridsdale was moved to another parish where more abuse occurred.

The Catholic Church failed in the duty of care to our boys and many others around Victoria. Their lost childhood, their struggle to maintain a normal life could have been avoided if Bishop Mulkearns, Head of the Catholic Church in Ballarat and Father George Pell (now Cardinal George Pell) who was a member of the College of Consultors (a group of priests who advised Mulkearns) had listened to even one complaint. I wonder what the boys' life might have been if their paths hadn't met with Ridsdale's.

I live with the guilt that it was me who sent the boys off to a Catholic School where a monster waited for more victims. I was a Catholic. My husband wasn't, but he was supportive of me when I wanted a Catholic education for the children. Who could imagine what was to follow? If only Bishop Mulkearns had listened, my journey and the boys' journey in life would have been different.

We attended the Victoria Inquiry in the Handling of Child Abuse by Religious Organisations (2012) and the Royal Commission into the Sexual Abuse of Children (2014). We requested a private verbal hearing with complete confidentiality. We spoke of the Ripple Effect in families. We are secondary victims. We struggle to hold a dysfunctional family together, to survive from day to day, waiting for that phone call late at night, wondering when the next crisis will be. The enormity of it all is not known by many. Their abuse is a silent sorrow. Confidentiality is important to our family, the boys still remain anonymous and they will carry their dark secret to their grave.

In 2013, there was a meeting in Ballarat we were invited to by Detective Sergeant Kevin Carson. He has been a great support to us and understands the nightmare of sexual abuse and the impact it has on secondary victims. We listened to Helen Last, who spoke about the Royal Commission and how important it was to put in a submission. Then a tall, well-spoken lady was introduced. Carmel Moloney spoke of a great life as a convert going to church with her husband, playing golf, working at St John of God hospital. She spoke of how she had heard of sexual abuse in the church, but it didn't affect her.

Then a friend told her about the sexual abuse her son had suffered, so Carmel started to seek more information and realized the enormity of the pain and struggle the victims were having, with no-one listening. The Catholic Church continued to make things difficult for the victims, and so began Carmel's journey to help all the victims she could by forming a small group called, Moving Towards Justice.

My fight to get help or to be heard had been hopeless. I listened to her speak and wondered where she had been 10 years ago when I so needed help and someone to talk to. But it is not until someone close to you is sexually abused that it becomes real, and you realise it did happen. I introduced myself and we have become firm friends. This amazing woman heard my story and has given me understanding and encouragement to be proud of what I have achieved for my family and other victims. Carmel's empathy, understanding and friendship continues. Carmel invited me to do a square for the Quilt of Hope. My square is Hope of a happy ending.

The boys' journey in life has been shaped by sexual abuse at an early age and they were later diagnosed with post-traumatic stress disorder (PTSD). They are very protective of their families. They fear pity and don't want to be known as victims or survivors. They struggle but with fierce determination they strive to maintain a normal life. There is a certain resilience about them. Our daughter has a great strength. She has a supportive husband and is a wonderful role model to her children. My admiration and love for her is boundless. It is a struggle for her to maintain a relationship with her brothers but with the love she has for her family she continues to try.

In 2003 Diane wrote:

We are happy in our ways, but as mum, dad, and three children I think we are a dysfunctional family. This should not be so, as I have a wonderful family and a husband who works hard to provide for his family who will move heaven and earth for our health and happiness. As a mother I can see in the eyes of my children the struggle life has become. They have moved away from time to time to be away from our family circle as they are aware of the tension in the family and this saddens me. We should not struggle to have a happy family life but the continuous pain the children carry and the emotional heart ache I feel each and everyday. My dream started out wonderful but has slowly died.

In November 2019, Diane reflects on her family situation:

The nightmare is still there, the sadness remains. I am seventy now and married fifty years. The children are married; there are grandchildren; there is some peace. I lost my faith but now I have found a balance. We are a resilient family. We as parents will continue to love our children unconditionally. I have learnt with my husband by my side that each day is a new day and we are still here holding on by a thread. We are proud of our children and all their achievements against great adversity. We are a family with great resilience, me up front, the children and their families in the middle and my husband in the background with his strong steady hand of unconditional love, strength and devotion holding our family together. His pain is just as great and is suffered in silence.

I feel very overwhelmed as I write and think about what I am writing the memories come flooding back…the struggle, the heartache, the pain, and sorrow we carry in silence, the disbelief that sexual abuse did happen by the clergy, the cover up by the church, the not wanting to believe that it happened to your children.

***

Once again, the memories come flooding back. The 9th of March 2022, the image of a court room a dark secret emerges again the headlines in today's paper "Ridsdale on Sexual Abuse Charges". Ridsdale was charged again and waiting on sentencing for abuse in the 1980s at Mortlake. The two victims are now in their 50s.

I said to my husband, "Forty years later the victims are still able to come forward and Ridsdale charged and sentenced for his crimes".

The Story of the Quilt of Hope

"Yes" he said, "we did that, we went to court and had the statute of limitations removed".

"Yes, I had forgotten that".

"All those memories we try and forget" he replied.

The story told – as I reflect on each paragraph, the discipline I had learnt to sleep at night, to carry on the next day and not let it consume me, was lost in this moment of time and the tears flowed. The constant struggle continues. The ripple effect continues. We remain secondary victims.

Chapter 6

A Mother's Fight for Justice
Helen Watson

In 1996, Helen Watson's 21-year-old son Peter told her that he had been sexually abused by a priest when he was 16. Three years later, Peter went missing after he absconded from a psychiatric facility. His body was discovered in a boat shed after completing suicide. Due to the inability to identify the body, it would be another six years before Helen learnt of his fate.

Helen's fight for justice for her son Peter has been relentless. Her anger at the inaction of the Catholic Church remains as does her heartache hearing the stories of others sexually abused by clergy. She witnessed the destruction of her son's life and experienced a multitude of personal battles.

Helen met Carmel at a gathering held at the Ballarat Yacht Club in 2013. The event had been planned to discuss the possibility of making the Quilt and inviting people to contribute to it.

The Story of the Quilt of Hope

Helen heard about the event from a work colleague, Irene, who was also a neighbour of Carmel's at the time. Helen had shared her story with Irene and each time they talked about it Irene was brought to tears. As noted by Helen, "It challenged her (Irene's) faith; she couldn't come to terms with Peter's sexual abuse and had lots of mixed emotions".

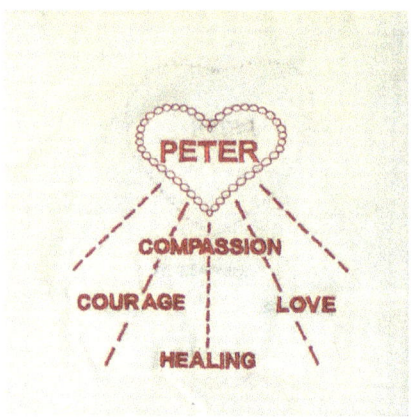

Row 7 Block 56
Made by Helen Watson

Row 9 Block 70
Unknown Maker

The block Helen embroidered has a heart encasing her son's name Peter with rays projected out amidst the words "compassion, courage, healing, love". The design and words represent the following:

Heart is holistic of the unconditional love I have for Peter.

Words of **compassion** and **courage** are strengths of Peter's character.

Healing and **love** are important for me to learn to live with this tragedy.

Helen's story is told using an abridged version of her submission to the Royal Commission into Institutional Response to Child Sexual Abuse

. Helen has written her story multiple times for different settings, and we agreed that using this content provided what was needed for this book.

It only touches the surface of her family's story. The complete and more detailed story may be told one day in the book Helen has been working on over the years.

***

My family

My mother was very committed to the Catholic Church. I was raised to respect God and the Church. I was educated in Catholic primary and secondary schools, and totally committed to my faith. My family and I lived and breathed Catholic religion.

In 1972, I married Tim Watson. From 1972 to about 1997, we lived on a farm in the small rural community of Tatyoon with our two sons, Peter and Michael. Our family travelled 40 kilometres to attend Mass at the Immaculate Conception Church in Ararat every Sunday. The boys grew up with the values of the Catholic faith, and both were altar boys. My son Peter went to Yalla-Y-Poora Primary School until Grade 6, when he moved to St Mary's Primary School in Ararat, Victoria.

Peter had a happy childhood and enjoyed playing football, cricket and basketball for the local community. He aspired to be a high achiever in all that he did. After primary school, Peter went to Marian College, which was right near the Ararat Presbytery.

In about 1991, I was volunteering in the canteen at Marion College. For some reason, I had to go to the Presbytery with a nun to collect supplies for the canteen. The Presbytery was next to the Church, which was next to the College. I remember that Father Paul David Ryan answered the door, reeking of alcohol. From this point onwards I will refer to him as Ryan because I hold no respect for him. This was the first time I met Ryan. I became aware that he was relieving Father Brendan Davey, who was the permanent Parish Priest in Ararat at that time.

Sleep over at the Presbytery

In 1991, when Peter was 16, Ryan invited him and some other boys to the Presbytery one night. Peter was invited to sleep over because he lived in the country and Ryan had agreed to bring him back home the next day. At the time, I felt honoured and proud that Peter was invited to stay at the Presbytery, so I agreed without hesitation.

The Sunday morning after the sleepover, Ryan brought Peter back home. I remember the day well, but not the date. I asked Ryan to come in and have some breakfast. He told me he had to go back and say Mass, which blew me away because he reeked of alcohol. After Ryan left, Peter went straight down to his room.

Sometime later, I was standing at the kitchen sink, and I looked out to see Peter in the paddock, probably 500 metres away. He was physically lifting logs that I did not believe any man could lift. He was building a bonfire. I wondered what was going on, so I went up to him to speak to him. Tears were rolling down his face and he just said, 'Go away, Mum. Go away, Mum.' So, I did. From that day onwards, Peter was different, and his behaviour changed. He withdrew into his room and became anti-social. He became very troubled, and started engaging in self-destructive behaviours, such as self-mutilation, drinking alcohol and then using drugs.

One day at school, Peter kicked down an ornate wooden staircase banister. Another time, Peter grabbed the bus driver around the throat. This kind of behaviour was really out of character. I didn't know what was wrong, I thought it might have just been adolescence. Remarkably, Peter completed schooling. He struggled, but he was quite an intelligent young lad.

After Peter left school, he just became transient. He left home and went to university for a year and worked part time at Nuts and Bolts in Altona. But soon he moved from place to place, lost touch with all his lifelong family and friends, and returned home only sporadically. He tried to work, but he was restless and unsettled and found it difficult to maintain employment.

Peter discloses the abuse

One day in 1996, when he was 21, Peter and I were driving from Tullamarine airport to the farm. During this trip, Peter told me that he had been sexually abused by a priest. He didn't say who this priest was. Peter then told me that if I told anyone about this, he would kill himself. I did not raise the subject again while we drove home.

Afterwards, I was torn between wanting to breach Peter's trust in me by confronting the Church about the sexual abuse, and not wanting Peter to take his life. That night my husband and I found Peter in bed with a loaded shotgun. This was Peter's first suicide attempt that I knew of. That night we took Peter to a psychiatric ward in Ballarat. After this, Peter needed frequent intervention from psychiatric services.

He started seeing a psychologist in Ballarat about the abuse. In 1997, my marriage with Tim broke down. Tim stayed on the farm, and I moved to Ararat. Peter lived between my house and the farm. Peter was still in and out of jobs, and in and out of psychiatric hospitals. He was also on marijuana and attempted to take his life on numerous occasions. There was a two-week period when Tim drove Peter to counselling sessions in Ballarat every day. I saw him struggle with the knowledge of what happened to Peter.

During this time, I was continually told by Peter's therapists that he had a pre-disposition to drugs and suffered from drug-induced psychosis. However, from living with Peter, I suspected that he had schizophrenia. Peter eventually told me that Ryan was the Priest who had sexually abused him. He told me that when he went to the Presbytery with Ryan and five or six other boys, Ryan gave the boys alcohol and they watched blue movies and then all played the card game 'Strip Jack' and ran around naked. Later that evening, the other boys went home, leaving Peter and Ryan alone in the Presbytery. Ryan was naked and ran a bath for Peter. He sexually abused Peter, and then they slept in the same bed until the following morning. Father Brendan Davey later told me that Peter used to get off the bus on his way to school, and smoke with Ryan at the Presbytery. He also said that Peter and other boys used to go to the Presbytery at lunch times for a smoke.

Peter goes missing

On 18 March 1999, Peter went to the Grampians where he thought about cutting off his penis and throwing himself over a cliff. He didn't. Instead, he went to his aunt's house where she told him he needed help and that he should go to the psychiatric hospital. Peter went and was admitted to the Grampians Psychiatric Unit in Ballarat. There he was involuntarily committed.

The hospital rang me to tell me that he had been committed. They also said that Peter had been diagnosed with schizophrenia and other mental health conditions. When I heard this, I thought, 'Thank God.' I had fought for years to get that diagnosis. Ten or fifteen minutes later, the hospital rang me back and said that Peter had absconded. They told me that he had asked to move his car, which was parked outside the hospital. He had tried to leave in his car. When it didn't start, he got out and smashed it up. Then he ran away.

Peter did not contact me after this. As a mother, I knew that he had come to some grief because he almost always contacted me when he was at his lowest. After Peter went missing, in desperation, I went to the Ararat Presbytery to report the sexual abuse by Ryan, and to seek help. I spoke with a nun. I cannot remember her name. I was crying and out of control. The nun said, 'Well you know, you are clearly not coping. We'll organise some counselling for you'. The church organised counselling in Ballarat for me and I went to the St John of God Hospital. I remember having a counselling session there and I think I went back for another session.

Soon after, Father Brendan Davey, the Parish Priest at that time, visited me at home in Ararat. He apologised for the abuse and said that he had no idea that it had happened. He also said that although there was something different about Ryan, he would not have thought that he was a sex offender. He didn't say what was different about Ryan.

Father Davey told me that he was not in the Parish when Ryan abused Peter. Later in 1999, I called Ballarat Police and spoke with a Detective. It was a pretty short conversation, but I told him my son's name, and that he had been sexually abused by Father Paul David Ryan in Ararat Parish when he was a teenager. I told him Peter had gone missing. A Detective said, 'I'll follow it up'. I didn't hear back from that Detective. I never followed it up because my life at that time was hell. I had to find Peter; the police were the least of my worries.

After my contact with the Church in 1999, I spent the next 6 years looking for Peter. I was beside myself and finding my son was my priority. I hoped that he would be alive, but I sort of knew that he would be dead. It was heartbreaking because I just knew that he had come to grief. I was in survival mode. During this time, the police contacted me from time to time because they had found bodies. I had to go in twice and make a statement. Neither of these bodies were Peter.

Peter's body is found

In December 2005, Senior Detective Constable John Jess from Ballarat Police visited me at home to tell me that Peter's body had been identified by a remarkable fingerprint match.

I later learned that on 20 October 1999, a woman had walked past a boat shed in Aspendale, Victoria, and smelt something. She got her husband, and they looked in the shed and saw a body hanging in there. The body was naked and painted blue. We didn't know until much later that the body was Peter. A police officer investigated, and concluded that it was death by suicide, and that the suicide had happened in about June of that year. The body was decomposed, and could not be identified, but a partial fingerprint was taken from a paint tin that was in the shed.

A series of missing person bulletins was published, but only in the Aspendale metropolitan area. The connection with Peter's disappearance wasn't made because the bulletins didn't come to Ballarat. Peter's body was not identified, and after a coronial inquest, he was buried as an unknown person in the Melbourne Necropolis.

About six years later, in 2005, the Police Officer in charge of the initial investigation in Aspendale, Senior Sergeant Rod Owen, was learning how to use new fingerprint identification technology from the United States. He tested the fingerprints of the unknown body with other prints on record, and Peter's fingerprints came up as a match.

He told me that he had always been troubled about the unidentified body in Aspendale and felt he must have had a family somewhere. When the police told me they had found Peter's body, I was sceptical at first because there had been so many wrong hits over the years. Once it was confirmed, we had to fight to have Peter's body exhumed. We couldn't exhume the body without a death certificate, and we had to have another coronial inquest to get a death certificate. I felt like we had to fight every step of the way.

Eventually we had Peter's body exhumed, and he was respectfully buried in the community cemetery, close to the family home at Tatyoon.

*Row 7 Block 49
Unknown Maker*

*Row 6 Block 45
Unknown Maker*

The Diocese's response

After Peter's body had been identified, I approached the Ballarat Diocese again. I met with Bishop Peter Connors on 21st February 2006. During this meeting, I told him that Ryan had sexually abused Peter. Bishop Connors responded in a muffled, monotone voice, "Not him again". I asked for a letter of apology, and for the Church to cover the costs of Peter's funeral in December 2005. I also told Bishop Connors that I wanted every bit of information he had on Ryan. He went over to the filing cabinet and shuffled around for a bit. He then told me that he did not have any records on Ryan in his office.

The day after I spoke with Bishop Connors, I was contacted by a Detective in Warrnambool investigating Ryan in relation to a complaint of child sexual abuse. I told him about my visit to Bishop Connors and that he had said there were no documents. I understand that this Detective applied for a search warrant and got documents from the Diocese relating to Father Ryan.

Father Ryan was later convicted of child sexual abuse offences against other boys. On 3 March 2006, I met with Bishop Connors again. I asked for counselling, which Bishop Connors agreed to. I insisted that I go to a counsellor of my choice, and Bishop Connors agreed. Between March and May 2006, the Church paid for me to go to 15 sessions of counselling.

On 20 March 2006, Bishop Connors wrote to me and offered, as a matter of pastoral concern, to provide financial assistance to cover the costs of Peter's burial. In this letter, Bishop Connors also acknowledged, and apologised for, Ryan's abuse of Peter. In June 2006, the Church gave me $10,679 to cover Peter's funeral expenses and the costs of exhuming Peter's body.

On 7 June 2006, I met with Bishop Connors and asked for compensation from the Church for the sexual abuse of Peter, and its impact on me. Counselling did not seem to be working and I was desperate to get help for myself. Bishop Connors told me that he was sorry about my son and that I may never get my faith back, but the Church had no money and I needed to take some responsibility for my own healing. I was shattered. I remember leaving the building in a highly emotional state. I felt as though the Church did not care about me, my struggle with the sexual abuse of Peter, or the loss of my son.

During 2008 and 2009, my counsellor contacted the Diocese and asked them to pay for further counselling sessions for me. The Diocese agreed, and approved counselling sessions. In May 2009, I met with Bishop Connors again, and he agreed to fund 10 more counselling sessions. After this, I did not approach the Church again until 2013, when Bishop Paul Bird was on board.

I first met with Bishop Bird on 3 December 2013. During this meeting I told him that I wanted recognition and compensation for my pain and suffering and counselling. We agreed that I would arrange a further meeting with Bishop Bird to discuss compensation. On 18 December 2013, I met again with Bishop Bird. He suggested that we try and resolve the issue of compensation through mediation.

Mediation

On 11 February 2014, I participated in a mediation with Bishop Bird and a mediator from South Australia. We had a morning session where I spoke about how I was feeling. I said that in my opinion the Church had minimised everything that had happened and that all they did was offer counselling. In the afternoon session, Bishop Bird said, 'Now, I want you to tell me how we can help you to heal'. And I said, 'I want to take 6 months off work to write a book because it is very therapeutic to record your thoughts, feelings and experiences. I definitely need counselling and the way I am feeling now, it might be for ten years. And, because I struggle with depression and anxiety, maybe some Tai Chi. I believe that would be helpful.' And he said, 'Yes'. The outcome of the mediation was amazing. It was a really good mediation.

In earlier meetings with Bishop Bird, I felt that he had been defensive, but he was totally different in the mediation. He told me that he had never realised the seriousness of the situation, or what I had been through. At the mediation, it appeared to me that he had tears rolling down his face. He said, 'I am sorry about all this.' I thought, 'Oh, well, that is his apology'. I walked away from the mediation feeling okay. I thought, 'I can now get my life back. I am going to be okay'. At the end of the mediation, Bishop Bird said, 'I'll get the Church's solicitor to contact your lawyer'. I gave Bishop Bird the name of my lawyer. I understood the lawyers would talk about the amounts of compensation we had discussed during the mediation. I contacted my lawyer, about a week after the mediation. He told me he had not been contacted by the Diocese or their lawyers.

Row 8 Block 59
Unknown Maker

Row 10 Block 74
Unknown

Civil claim

In April or March 2014, my solicitor Mr Hills contacted the Church's lawyers to advise them of my intention to make a civil claim against the Catholic Diocese of Ballarat. We hadn't heard from the Church's lawyers after the mediation.

I felt I had to go down the civil path because nothing came of the mediation. I couldn't walk away. Over the following months, I had three psychiatric assessments. On 4 December 2014, Mr Hills, my barrister Tim Seccull and I met with Patrick Monahan, who I understood was the Diocese's lawyer, in Melbourne. During the mediation, I waited outside the room because I decided not to meet the Diocese's lawyer. I don't know whether that was the right thing to do or not. The Diocese offered me $40,000 in compensation and said this was because I had already been given about $11,000 for counselling and for the costs of Peter's burial. My niece, who came to the mediation as a support person, told me not to accept this offer because that amount would not even cover counselling. There was no settlement at that mediation. My civil claim is still unresolved.

Police investigations

In 2013, I gave evidence at the *Victorian Inquiry into the Handling of Child Abuse by Religious and Other Organisations*[1]. As a result of this Inquiry, a police officer was assigned to properly investigate what happened to Peter, including his death. I was very happy with this outcome.

My ex-husband Tim spoke to Detective Senior Constable David Rae from SANO Taskforce, who was working on our case. As a result, in April 2014, Tim and I both made statements to the police about Peter's abuse by Ryan. However, we know that Ryan can't be prosecuted for his abuse of Peter because Peter is dead and there is no hard evidence.

Last year, my son Michael and I went to see Father Brendan Davey. My son asked Father Davey whether he thought Ryan had abused Peter. He said yes. When we asked why he thought that, Father Davey said it was because a Detective had told him. I also went to St John of God Hospital, and there was no record of me going to counselling there.

Impact on my life and my family

While Peter was alive, I struggled daily supporting him and watching him struggle with life after the sexual abuse. I watched his life spiral out of control. Peter had been an intelligent, gentle, fun loving and beautiful soul. He was respected by all who knew him.

After the abuse, he felt worthless, lacked motivation, and had low self-esteem with bouts of depression. Peter's tragic journey following the sexual abuse started with escalating antisocial behaviours.

Our family became fractured due to Peter's journey of self-destruction, and my marriage with Tim broke down. I started gambling and drinking alcohol. I threw myself into my work because I didn't want to think about what happened. Work, gambling and drinking were my coping mechanisms. I have had feelings of tremendous guilt that I couldn't protect my son.

Peter was adopted and I have tried to contact his birth mother, but I haven't been able to. I feel I have let her down. I continue to experience a great sense of loss. I have lost my son, my family, my faith and my happiness. I have endured this struggle for the last 20 years because of the sexual abuse of my son by Ryan.

Apart from the tragedy of what happened to my family, the events also had an impact on my faith. I have lost my faith, which was historically a huge part of my life. I have also lost my trust in the Church because I felt that it protected the offender but did nothing to protect the victims. I still hold that view today. I feel like I am stuck in this system where the Catholic Church has absolute total control. What do I do? Do I walk away? I can't walk away because I'm not healed, and there has been no justice for Peter.

I retired in October 2014. I had a good working career, but when I retired the reality of life hit me big time. I am now receiving counselling and it is the first time that counselling is actually working and has ever really been successful.

I believe that Ryan and the Catholic Church destroyed my son. I think that the beliefs of his Catholic education and the Church and our family values, all instilled in him since childhood, prevented him from reporting the abuse. Peter never said anything against Ryan, even after he disclosed the abuse.

***

Helen writes in 2022

The impact of the Royal Commission (RC) had on me was immense. Reading my impact statement was heart wrenching beyond belief. Then sitting in that court room day after day listening to and watching victims provide accounts of their sexual abuse by catholic clergy. All so different but each victim's statement was cruel and sickening knowing what they had been through and still to this day struggle with day to day living.

Once my RC subpoena had expired, I could not attend any more sittings. I was a mess emotionally and physically. It was then that I decided to move from Ballarat to hopefully avoid contact with people who were a constant reminder of the atrocious acts of the Catholic Church who protected their offending clergy enabling the abuse of our vulnerable young males to continue. I relocated to Beaufort and tried to become more grounded than I had been over many many years when this nightmare began in the late 1990s.

It has been a huge journey to rid myself of the maladaptive behaviours of alcohol and poker machine dependence. I had extensive counselling to address this which led me to entering a rehab program in Geelong. Two weeks of hell. Then with the help of a counselling psychologist, I started to live with mindfulness which has been life changing for me. Mind you I still bear the scars of the past, but the mindfulness approach helps me when I struggle.

I still hang onto the words of wisdom from the police officer who arrested Ryan. He said to me way back then to "get fire in your belly Helen". There were many times I thought everything was too hard, but I did keep the fire in my belly and still have it to give me strength when need be.

I have been a shell of a person, not my body but my soul was gone. They raped my soul.

I see myself as a tenacious mother who never gave up trying to get justice for my son Peter and other victims. In my attempts to advocate for victims I have been quite vocal through the media over the years and was able to do this because I had "fire in my belly".

I have met many amazing people during this journey and am thankful for their support and friendship.

Endnotes

1. https://www.parliament.vic.gov.au/images/stories/committees/fcdc/inquiries/57th/Child_Abuse_Inquiry/Transcripts/Helen__Tim_Watson_07-Dec-12.pdf

A quilt was made for Helen in remembrance of Peter. It contains multiple photos of her son and one of his shirts was incorporated throughout the quilt.

Chapter 7

Memoirs of a Catholic School Teacher

Ann Ryan

Ann Ryan was a primary school teacher at St Colman's Parish School in Mortlake, Victoria from 1973 until 1996. It was during her time there that Father Gerard Risdale, as the parish priest, permeated the community and abused numerous boys that she had taught within her classroom during 1981 and 1982. It was not until Ridsdale left the parish after 18 months that she began to learn of the atrocities committed by him and the complicity of the Catholic Church.

Years of seeking justice for the families of Mortlake and their children, including multiple communications with Bishop Mulcearns and the continued silence of the Church, prompted Ann to send a letter to twenty-one priests across the Ballarat Diocese. The letter appealed for collective action to be taken by spiritual leaders in the diocese to address the impacts of clerical child sexual abuse. With little response to this, Ann sent further letters to other parts of the Catholic Church hierarchy to no avail. Despite advocating further in the public realm, the responses received were dismissive and no action was taken by Church authorities.

Ann chose a Brigid's Cross to be embroidered on her block for the Quilt of Hope. This symbol holds great significance to Ann and was selected to represent her journey "for truth, justice and hope".

As a teacher at the school and parish member, she shares her lived experience of this time and the harrowing journey of relentlessly advocating for her students and their families. Her powerful and confronting story reveals the emotional struggle to comprehend what had occurred within her community and the unfathomable apathy of a Church in which she had held faith throughout her life.

What follows is an excerpt from Ann's memoirs which at the time of publication were in the final stages of being completed.

***

Ann Begins her Tale: Easter 1 April 2018

"My name is Ann and I have lived my entire life, except for two years, in the Catholic Diocese of Ballarat. I lived a very active Catholic life until 1997, when the flame died forever. I loved the teachings of the Gospels and believed them to the depths of my soul. I attended Sacred Heart Teachers' College here in Ballarat and taught in Catholic schools in this diocese for 28 years! It seems fitting that I am here, once again, in Ballarat, to speak to this Inquiry ... I am so grateful for such an opportunity because, hopefully, we are now moving towards truth, justice, peace and some kind of recovery!

I come to speak for the boys I taught. Boys I taught whilst being unaware of the dire situation many of them were in at the time. I am their voice: seeking a hearing, being believed, achieving some degree of justice at last. Seeking empathy for their struggles, as they live their lives amongst family and friends. The years from 1982-1997 were personally fraught with anguish, calling for help from the church authorities; namely the bishop of the diocese, the Diocesan Pastoral Council; the Council of Priests; the Special Issues Committee - through letters, personal visits, participation in Diocesan Planning and events. It was a call to challenge, and begging almost, but the responses were manifestly devoid of any genuine feeling for the victims.

Row 2 Block 16
Made by Kaye Leckie for Ann Ryan

Row 5 Block 37
Made by Anne O'Çonnell

I need to ask again. "Why did the Bishop, the Council of Priests, the Special Issues Committee, the Diocesan Pastoral Council, the 1994 Diocesan Assembly ...... all the representative bodies of the people of the Ballarat Diocese ... why did they not hear the depth and enormity of what was taking place? Why did they not act to protect and care for all vulnerable children who had no voice? Why did they respond so remotely and coldly to my efforts? Why did the Sisters of Mercy not take more appropriate action at the time?" And, more than anything, I still wonder at the continuous and thunderous 'silence' of catholic communities!

And so, at the Ballarat Hearing on 28th February 2013, I introduced myself to the committee members of the Victorian Parliamentary Inquiry into the Handling of Child Abuse by Religious and other Non-government Organisations, operating from April 2012-November 2013 and culminating in a final report aptly titled 'Betrayal of Trust'.[1]

How had a moderately shy and unassuming Catholic teacher found herself such an auspiciously public forum? A place where truth was the driver and the Committee was witness to its unbelievable secrets. I was that teacher and little did I realise on that astonishing day, that just three years hence, the experience would be repeated at Melbourne's County Court on 16 December 2015, before the Commissioner of the Royal Commission into Institutional Responses to Child Sexual Abuse. The Royal Commission would deliver its Final Report based on the revelation of unimaginable truths on 16 December 2017.

For years now I have been inexplicably drawn to, and fascinated by, Edvard Munch's painting, "The Scream". Being born with a keenly active social conscience, I saw it as definitively representing pain, personal pain, even the pain of the world. I could hear that scream inside my head! And perhaps it does represent all of those things. But in more recent years, it definitely represents, to my mind, the pain of traumatised children, on the brink of insanity.

And it causes me to weep.

Little children, innocents, spirit and soul taken away by other human beings ... the brutalisation which was allowed to continue through collective denial. Little children who had no power against those authorities with huge power over communities; but who had no power over the silence of the communities themselves!

Over many years, I sought justice for my students. Unbeknown to me, these young children, whilst under my duty of care, were being defiled through subjection to the most evil and criminal actions of a paedophile priest. I simply acted as I thought any Catholic would under similar circumstances. I acted from the heart, driven by the gospel values of truth and justice espoused by Jesus' teachings.

I did indeed challenge Church authority, but as a believer, and from within. I did not leave the Church readily or with haste. I endeavoured to address the problem around my demonic discovery by exposing child sexual abuse through active engagement with numerous internal Diocesan Church structures. I looked for support and appropriate responses. But alas, the institution did not want to hear me.

The ensuing years of long and lonely pilgrimage unmasked an ethical juxtaposition. I encountered a sinister, dysfunctional and amoral world. It was completely Pharisaic; it was filled with medievalism, indifference and extreme apathy. It thrived on defensive strategies borne out of the ancient depths of canon law, blatant lies and cover-up. All the energy was directed at saving face. It has become clear that the church can no longer be associated with the principles of honour.

Thus, I embarked on my extremely alienating journey which, for sanity's sake, I embraced as 'pilgrimage'. For as long as I can recall, I have reflected on life as 'pilgrimage', one's very existence being about journeying forever seeking a higher consciousness. This 'pilgrimage', however, slowly and painfully brought about the demise and destruction of my Catholic faith, which had been the cornerstone of my living for so long, directing so much of my thinking and action. And continuing to drive this particular 'pilgrimage' is, not only the collective abandonment of those children, but the deafening COLLECTIVE SILENCE of the Catholic Church community, from grassroots to the Curia.

The Story of the Quilt of Hope

Throughout this very personal pilgrimage, and especially during its beginning years whenever I freely expressed my lived reality, the emotional depth of my pain was too overwhelming at times, even for family and close friends. I could find no-one to share my outrage and join me in action, not even Church clerics! I could not understand! We were talking of children being raped then being expected to exist invisibly in a living hell whilst the adults of their lives were unable to group together and demand justice.

I was searching for support and positive action, but it was not forthcoming. Most I spoke with found the situation unfathomable and found my thinking and allegations impossible. Such constant and unsupportive responses caused me to withdraw my emotional self. I needed to sustain any remaining sanity but most especially, to care for both my spirit and my soul. The beautiful humanist, Nelson Mandela, proclaimed so succinctly the essence of community. *'There can be no keener revelation of a society's soul than the way in which it treats its children'.* ... I will never understand the collective inaction I witnessed! *Never!*

And so, this personal pilgrimage intensified. I was destined to carry on the search for truth and justice in a manner that was almost clandestine in nature. I had stepped into a labyrinthine world of revelations, resistance and disbelief. The more I uncovered, the greater became those numbers of children, the greater became the extent of the perpetration! At first you can hardly believe what is happening; how will you negotiate the madness? My heart weighed heavy as lead and was wrapped so tightly in grief and remains so. How could this story be told?

Pour moi, it was an unrequested challenge, a social responsibility. It must be told for the sakes of all the little children brutally treated and unheard, to honour the pain, struggle and courage of victims, survivors, families and advocates; to raise matters of truth accompanied surely by some increased level of critical thinking about the governance and culture of institutions, especially, and statistically, the worst institutional offender, the Catholic Church.

The truth of so many human atrocities remains hidden from the collective narrative. The truth of this particular story demands to be recorded in history, because it reveals, in its scope and effect, such a legacy of evil, of such human destruction ... visited upon innocent children.

The Day the Music Died!

1981 and from my perspective, life within the school seemed to be as it should; nothing untoward! However, this was the year that heralded the arrival of some decidedly dark and intense times; years where evil and its aftermath would rain down upon my child students, myself and all those especially connected to the Catholic community of St Colman's Parish, Mortlake, Victoria. This was the year in which that community received a *'gift'* from the diocesan authorities in the form of a new parish priest: Gerald Ridsdale. He would remain in parish ministry for the next eighteen months; such a short term, but one that was destined to carry horrendously long-term damage!

Who was this man? I knew of this priest from his years at St Joseph's Parish Church in Warrnambool. However, I was ignorant of his unbelievable propensity for crime until October 1982! It was at that juncture that a new pathway was laid down for me. Years of fervent faith and dedication dissolved into a pain-filled journey laden with expanding and deepening disbelief which created an appalling time of relentless and desperate struggle. Gerald Ridsdale, parish priest and therefore, employer, never once attended our weekly staff meetings in all the time he was amongst us. Nor did he engage much at all with teachers - an aspect that didn't particularly perturb me as I had no interest in being in the presence of this man. He was a physically large man and used this to his advantage, presenting, in my view, as both arrogant and dismissive. However, the wider adult community seemed entranced by his creative and interesting ways of engaging children, especially with regards to all things religious; calling them around the altar; maintaining the fervour was everything! I always considered him a truly fine example of what it is to be a *'strutter'*!

Whether it was late 1981, but most assuredly during 1982, I noted markedly disturbing behavioural changes in most of the Year 5-6 boys. Sexually driven talk, jokes, ravenous perusal of books such as encyclopedia and dictionaries ... almost incessant! Clearly abnormal behaviour for the age group. Responding to my sense of duty of care I discussed the concerning changes with Sister Kate. Whilst acknowledging my concerns, she was unable to offer any reasonable explanations. So we agreed to view the extraordinary sexual interest and its attached behaviour as an untimely elevation in natural curiosity or indeed early onset of puberty! But the boys' behaviour held such a collaborative quality; an affinity which should have alerted us to dismiss such naïve notions as those we had settled on.

From a teacher's perspective, another troubling aspect of this time was centred around the responsibility of *'doing yard duty'*. During recess times the Years 5-6 boys would simply disappear from the schoolyard and go to the presbytery. Gerald Ridsdale had set his rooms up with games such as a pool table and the newly available Atari video games. Because those with the knowledge remained silent, these curious and fun-loving young boys around the Ballarat diocese went like lambs to the slaughter. I cannot begin to understand why we, as teaching staff, did not ask questions of the principal regarding these *'out of the schoolyard'* visits. Perhaps we discussed it amongst ourselves and because of the high regularity with which it took place, perhaps we concluded that the boys had their teachers' permission. What prevented us from pursuing the answer? Why did we presume? The truth of the answer as we know it today would have been unconscionable.

Monsignor Leo Fiscalini was now parish priest of St Thomas' Parish in Terang and, when a family whose children attended St Colman's School, Mortlake, discovered one of their sons had suffered very serious sexual violence at the hands of Ridsdale, they, as dedicated people of faith, visited the Monsignor for support and guidance. Both family and boy were urged to keep it quiet *'for the church's sake*'! I do believe that a now deceased local GP also made efforts at a diocesan level to have the atrocity dealt with, but I am unaware of any outcome. Within the decade, Fiscalini would go on to facilitate further cover ups of paedophilic crimes. This included those of his assistant priest, Paul David Ryan, after his return from one of his many, diocesan-funded *'study trips'* to America.

I now know that there is no doubt that Sister Kate McGrath knew more than she was sharing with me or any member of staff. I was to discover thirty-two years later, in 2013, during the life of the Victorian Parliamentary Inquiry, that she had already endured the presence of this monster, now amongst us, in her Edenhope life, prior to coming to Mortlake. Little wonder, that on his arrival, her anxieties and apprehensions about this priest were renewed.

Returning to Ballarat and I reconnected with Kate in 2013. She had yet another harrowing story from that time between Ridsdale's dismissal and the close of the 1982 school year. In desperation and distress, she had planned, along with some of the affected parents, to travel to Camperdown to confront Bishop Ronald Mulkearns, who was due in town to bestow the Sacrament of Confirmation. However, none of the parents materialised, so she travelled alone to seek support for the sexually abused children. She put the question and he delivered his reply, which now rests securely archived within the documented transcripts of both the Victorian Parliamentary Inquiry and the Royal Commission: His emphatic reply was, *'There will be nothing done for the children, as that would be admitting guilt'*. No doubt Kate turned towards Mortlake with a heavy and disconsolate heart, having been 'sworn to silence' yet again. Her complicity in the cover-up was reinforced. How would she begin to cope with such an issue, alone?

My not so misty memory tells me it was a day in late October 1982, as little more than a week earlier, on 17 October, our son had received the Sacrament of First Communion, administered by Gerard Risdale, whom we now recognise as a paedophile priest and criminal, any inner strife being carried by Kate was on the brink of being exploded. A student's mother arrived at the classroom door in an extremely distressed state, indicating to Sister Kate that Ridsdale was abusing all the boys.

Row 6 Block 42
Made by Maureen Burke

Row 9 Block 69
Unknown Maker

I really do want to believe that the world fell in for Kate, that it was her moment of truth *absolute*! She certainly does admit to being horrified and shocked beyond belief and after spending time with the distraught mother, she approached the head of the Mortlake Sisters of Mercy community, Sr Patricia Vagg, parish pastoral worker. As I recall the detail as told to me by Sr Patricia Vagg years later, her position of responsibility for the religious community meant that it was she who must face the devil himself and lay the charges at his feet. She indicated that it took some considerable effort to get Ridsdale to admit to the allegations and when he did so she insisted that he call Bishop Mulkearns, otherwise she would. He made the call while Kate called the parents of her students.

In fact, it was not Bishop Mulkearns who was called but the Vicar-General, Henry Nolan, a highly respected and well-liked Mortlake parish priest of the immediate past. It was he who had to facilitate the monster's removal and, although he knew so many parish families intimately, he made no pastoral movement towards anyone. Nothing was facilitated for the victims or parish. It was all about the perpetrator. The nuns were sworn to silence. I believe that at that time, the younger teaching sister of the community may have been kept ignorant of the truth, as most parishioners had been! The Mortlake cover-up had started right there!

Over the next few days there was a very hurriedly organised *'phone around* farewell arranged for Gerald Ridsdale. Unusually it was scheduled for a week-day evening and set to be held in the parish hall. Without thinking too much about the reasons, and as I was part of the teaching staff, our family attended, along with quite a small number of parishioners. We had been invited, but still did not suspect that we were indeed being drawn towards anything unusual or sinister. Usually, a priest's farewell was a daytime event which was well promoted weeks ahead. We were blind, and before we could see, he was gone! The coverup was taking shape!

Masses the following weekend were celebrated by Monsignor F.J. McKenzie, a retired priest with family connections to the district, a priest who often filled in when needed. Because he was known to the parish community and had our trust, we had no reason to question his statement when he gave us the news; we believed him. I should qualify that assertion and say, those of us who were unaware of the truth believed him! He told us, from the altar, that Father Gerry was experiencing severe grief after having lost a family member to death and that it was not known when he would return. Those who did know the truth knew that this priest would never return to our parish and were therefore complicit in deceiving the parish community.

Following that Mass and whilst standing within a circle of Catholic parish women, including school mothers, my world as I had known it, began to collapse around me. I have never looked on humanity in quite the same way since. The erosion of trust began in that moment. Even now I can see their faces. As part of the conversation, I had remarked on the difficulties our parish priest was having, only to receive the reply, *'Oh Ann, don't be so naïve!'* *'What do you mean?'* Covert glances before someone says, *'He's been interfering with the boys.'* Again *'What do you mean?'* Then, so derisively, *'Ann, you are sooooooooooooooooo naïve!'*

During our conversation it became clear that the wider Mortlake community already had an indication of the evil potential of this priest. Apparently, sometime in 1981, visiting Edenhope lawn bowlers, after establishing that Ridsdale was indeed the new parish priest in the town warned, *'You need to watch your young boys!'* I could elicit no answers, only silence! I curled into myself as if entering metamorphosis! This was the beginning day of a journey into the unknown, where I would truly come to experience and understand the fullness of silence and non-communication! *'Hello darkness, my old friend I've come to talk with you again ... And the vision that was planted in my brain, Still remains, within the sounds of silence'.* [Simon & Garfunkel] Conspiratorial, unshakeable silence! This, *pour moi*, was *'the day the music died!'*

There was nothing done for the children, and nothing done for the staff. We never knew the truth or the enormity of what we were amongst. We were denied, as teachers, any opportunity to attend to our responsibility, our duty of care. In casual conversations with other parishioners, I sometimes sprung unexpected questions in desperate attempts to discover which families may have been affected by Ridsdale. However, no-one seemed prepared to divulge any details. I read and researched all that I could about *'adults interfering with children'* and my world began its decline into greyness. I continued to teach, observe and wonder about the boys. I was continually tormented by such questions as, 'Who amongst you is hurt? How do you cope with each day? How do you concentrate on your learning? Is anyone doing anything specific to support your recovery? How can you, as a child, maintain such an outwardly normal persona?'

I could never give voice to my questions, as there was nowhere to take them! However, my little bit of newfound and ugly knowledge did help me to understand and handle more empathetically any troubling behaviour as it arose. Everyone, myself included, seemed to be living with the acceptance that something atrocious had taken place here. But no questions were asked! It just dwelt like a stagnant and unnamed monster amongst us. Silence reigned. It was as though not only the parish community, but the whole Mortlake community, had gone into consummate shutdown!

Inconceivable as it sounds, I have been assured that the Edenhope community shared a similar response. However, today, in that Western Wimmera Victorian town, people are more circumspect when they say collectively, and with conviction, that *'Ridsdale ruined Edenhope!'*

A Letter to the Priests

During my Catholic years I had always presumed that the many years of priestly training involved such a significant depth of extensive study, prayer and personal development in order to achieve some deeper and authentic understanding of what it is to be truly human. After all, these men would one day work as pastors of people, servants to humanity. And so, it was in 1993, carrying such a belief within my heart, and being so troubled as to where to turn next to gain some just outcomes for my Mortlake boys, that I turned to these men of the Ballarat Catholic diocese, the clergy, our priests, our holy men. I was confident that a collective letter, a copy of which was sent to each priest I knew or had at some time worked with, would surely ignite some outrage and action.

The nature of my letter being as it was, I imagined a major diocesan uprising, even class action. However, the class action that was to come in the years ahead belonged in quite a different context. As Gerald Ridsdale's very public first court hearing and conviction had taken place in that same year, I felt very confident that such a looming and troubled climate could not have escaped any discerning person's notice. Especially not the notice of those so totally dedicated to humanity, with all its sorrows and joys, as our diocesan priests.

Having been in continued and exasperated communication with Bishop Mulkearns for years, I decided in desperation and as a practising Catholic, to reach out to the priests as well, pleading for the little boys raped and assaulted by a now proven paedophile priest. I expected a compassionate and pastoral response. The full text of my October 1993 letter (refer to Appendix A) is provided in the hope of providing, especially for the uninitiated, some small insights into what was being requested of the diocesan priests, 28 years ago.

A copy of this letter, accompanied by another written by a Mortlake parent, was sent to twenty-one Ballarat Diocesan priests and each of the three Mortlake families who have shared their pain with me. The letter drew four replies and two phone calls. Bishop Ronald Mulkearns (27th October 1993) served only to benumb me…"What would Jesus have done?" I confess that I don't really know. I don't think the question is capable of a simple answer.

One of the phone calls received was from Father Patrick Downes from his Port Fairy presbytery. He was distressed and asked what he could possibly do to help and if I had knowledge of affected families. Through the conversation, we came to an agreed decision, and it was left to me to arrange a visit to Port Fairy for any interested parents. These parents were a part of a people he had grown to love and respect from his days of ministry as Mortlake's parish priest. So, after contacting the six affected parents I knew of, the proposed visit was confirmed and during one summer's night, just three of us made the journey to Port Fairy; travelling in a silence of anticipation but returning in a silence of weeping. In between these two very evocative periods of silence, Father Patrick Downes had not only embraced and held these parents, but cried openly in their presence, unable to offer any constructive help. I never saw or spoke to him again. There was no practical outcome and the next news I had of him was that he had contracted Parkinson's Disease and had returned to his beloved Ireland. It was revealed years later through the Royal Commission that he had been a member of the Bishop's Advisory Committee.

Row 3 Block 19
Unknown Maker

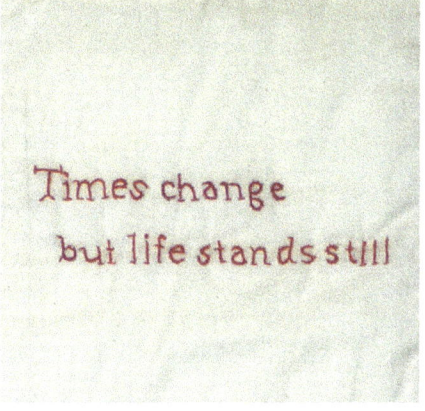

Row 6 Block 48
Lyn Snibson

The written reply from John McKinnon, suggested that the appropriate forum would be the Diocesan Council of Priests. Taking up this advice, I wrote a second lengthy letter and mailed it (along with a copy of the letter written by a Mortlake parent in October 1993) to the Council secretary Father Peter Sherman in January 1994. The mail out also included a copy of last October's letter for Father Sherman, as he was a non-respondent to the original. I sent the letters with confidence and hope that with luck the content of the two letters might draw curious attention from someone who had not been privy to the details of last October's letter. Snippets of my January 1994 letter are reproduced here.

In October of 1993 many priests received a letter from me expressing concern and hurt on behalf of myself, as a teacher and church member and some Mortlake families affected by the inappropriate actions of Gerry Ridsdale whilst he was parish priest of Mortlake … the concern expressed included the inaction of the institution in reaching out compassionately and practically to these victims, who you would be well aware are not restricted to Mortlake but are diocesan wide … the letter also included some ideas for action and healing within the Church … I was hopeful that a process of recognition and reconciliation could be initiated and implemented at diocesan level … today I place this hope in your hands, as our spiritual leaders, and pray that courage and compassion prevail. It is a big ask but I know it is a just ask!

I received a written response from Father Peter Sherman on 7th February 1994 which advised me that the Council of Priests was not scheduled to meet until '22 March and that I am sending a copy of the letters to Brian McDermott, the chairman, as we prepare the agenda for the meeting'.

Late April brought a reply from that March meeting indicating

'that the letter of 7 January was presented to the meeting of the Ballarat Diocesan Council of Priests … and that *'after respectfully listening to your letter and the letter of Mr. xxxxxxxxx, there's been* 'some general discussion and that the letter was to be referred on to the Special Issues Committee'.

Through this letter, the Council of Priests expressed *'concern for me and the issues you are trying to resolve and hope further contact will be made'.*

These priests, these holy men, were our spiritual leaders. Whilst their expressed concern was noted, it seemed as though the ball had been bounced right back at me! Not a skerrick of practical, constructive advice. 'Contact by whom?' Was the expectation that I just trundle on, single-handedly searching for appropriate resolution to such intrinsic and complicated issues? I had written on behalf of a community in pain, looking for them to show some leadership. How can you explain, to your diocesan community, your lack of leadership? Your perpetual silence? You need to understand that 'we' see it as betrayal, an avoidance of your pastoral duty of care. Consequently, in the ensuing weeks I contacted the Special Issues Committee mentioned in the letter of reply and, as the later months of 1994 closed in, I wrote once again to Church diocesan structures, sending copies to the Council of Priests, Bishop Mulkearns, the Special Issues Committee and the Interim Diocesan Pastoral Council.

My All Souls' Day 1994 letter showed a desperation towards breaking the silence: *'we have to demonstrate that we care'*. I suggested setting aside one weekend annually and in diocesan unison: *'for the promotion of reconciliation and healing of victims, families and parishes.'* I created a very simple liturgical format and accompanying prayer as an example of what might be considered. It incorporated themes of forgiveness, reconciliation and healing. *'We pray for the times we ignored the signs, for the times we ignored what we were told, for not being discerning people, for not reaching out, for not speaking out, for our apathy, for contributing to the silence, for denying truth, for disallowing justice.'* I did receive a response from Bishop Mulkearns, but not from the Diocesan Council of Priests; so, in the February of 1995 I sent a copy of the All Souls' Day letter to Father Peter Sherman, expressing concern that there'd been no reply and perhaps the original may not have been received!

Months on from the original All Souls' Day 1994 mailing, a letter arrived in my post box; dated Ash Wednesday 1995. It was written by Father Peter Sherman who wrote that he had indeed received and presented the November letter to the Council of Priests' meeting, from which he was directed to write to me. However, he apologised as he, "had overlooked to do so" He went on to say that

> *"there'd been a long and worthwhile discussion which raised many issues about the diocese ... the role of bishop, reconciliation, the effects*

of sexual abuse on individuals and its overall effect on the diocese ... this issue has touched many parishes in many different ways, from direct involvement to people being hurt about the bad media being received by the Church ... it was expressed at the meeting that there was a greater need for healing than reconciliation. If after healing there is still a need, then a reconciliation process comes into effect ... the group recommended that themes of healing and reconciliation be included in the Diocesan Call to Prayer throughout the year... the priests acknowledged that people are hurting from many things; divorces, people effected by the laws of the Church, the insensitivity of some Church pronouncements and that any reconciliation needs to cover a broad range of hurts, not only those who are victims of sexual abuse ... the Council did not recommend to the Bishop that he instigate such a weekend ... each parish is encouraged to do what it sees as appropriate for that place in the light of the Bishop's call for a year of prayer.'

'We' absolutely needed more than the power of prayer. It struck me that Church authorities are happy to place the initiative in the hands of the lay people when it suits them. My letter was not addressing any of those extra troublesome issues that have caused unnecessary misery to so many Catholics for eons. Nor was it addressing the bad media being received by the Church. The Church was receiving what it deserved. You just don't get it! My letter was attempting to address the 'elephant in the room', the issue of abandoned children and families, victims of child sexual abuse by priests, paedophile priests of this diocese. Within my thoughts of private response, strong, repressed feelings soared to the surface: exasperation, exhaustion, dejection, disgust, distress, vexation, weariness, being plain fed up and just sick and tired of the continuous blah, blah, blah!

My inner voice asked of the priests, 'How can you reconcile your souls?' My letters spoke of human beings and their never ending and unbelievable distress. They represented thousands of little children who would never grow into the fullness of their lives, of broken families, of criminal behaviour, not only on the part of paedophile priests, but including all those whose inaction and denial supported and sustained those dysfunctional priesthoods. Priests have been known to declare that *'victims of clergy abuse don't carry their pain alone'*, insinuating that they too carry some related pain. How could any priest hold such a thought as authentic, when collectively throughout the Ballarat diocese, they remained silent. They did not rise up, nor did they raise their voices in anger. The collective of diocesan priests merely turned their backs on little children in dire need of help.

Consequently, the Ash Wednesday 1995 letter moved me to abandon any hope of ever moving those priests from their seats of comfort and irrelevance. I was destined to discover alternative pathways. After the six weeks of Lent, Easter 1995 brought the long-awaited realisation home to my heart. I had truly lost all respect for the priests of the Ballarat Catholic Diocese, a diocese now known to have been riddled, for decades, for generations, with known paedophile priests such as John Day, John Leyden, Sydney Morey, Leonard Monk, Gerald Ridsdale, Paul David Ryan, Bryan Coffey, Robert Claffey and Leslie Sheahan. Their monstrous behaviour was further accentuated by the paedophile activity of religious teaching brothers such as Robert Best, Edward Dowlan, Gerald Fitzgerald, John Laidlaw, Stephen Farrell and Kenneth Paul McGlade. Since the close of the Royal Commission into Institutional Responses to Child Sex Abuse in December 2017, revelations have surfaced through legal proceedings, which strongly suggest that some diocesan paedophile priests and brothers were working together to conduct their criminal activity.

Because of inaction from within the church I began to use my voice more publicly. I had come to know some older young men who had been affected, and with them we contacted Broken Rites. I have continued to write letters to our local newspaper the Standard, whenever the opportunity arises. I participated in a Four Corners program in 1996 to try and raise issues and attended a public forum in Ballarat in the same year. I have personally supported a few of the young men that I came to know after the court hearing in

Warrnambool in 1994, when Gerard Ridsdale was tried. Two of these young men have since passed away. During this latter time of my particular struggle, in 1996, both the Principal and the Parish Priest connected to my parish and school actively threatened my teaching position if I continued in the public domain. So, I resigned from teaching in parish schools in 1996.

Row 9 Block 68
Made by Maxine Rouche

Row 1 Block 7
Made by Monica Gurry for
Fr Kevin Dillon

I have no regrets, as I am so convinced that adult communities will not come to fully realise the depth of depravity visited on their little children until the collective stories are told in strong, graphic language. To date, the language of the common lexicon has been far too soft, enabling adults to fling the revelations aside as a *'bit of tickling'* or *'horseplay'* as did another of Ballarat's diocesan paedophile priests, Les Sheahan, as he described his criminal actions. Responsible adults also need to see the brutalisations and rapes in the fullness of their appropriate contexts: that of a small, powerless, and bewildered child alone with a grown, virile man, being asked to do very unfamiliar things far beyond their understanding. People need to project the images of their own wee brains into victims' stories, then listen very carefully to the response from their own hearts. Maybe then, just maybe, we will witness a decline in adult apathy matched by a rise in adult empathy, accompanied by a fitting outrage.

The link to Brigid's Cross

It was a Saturday evening in June 1984. I was celebrating my thirty-seventh birthday with a lovely group of friends gathered at our home. Live music was provided by my friend Marie on piano and myself on violin, interspersed with copious amounts of Beatles, Joan Baez and Bob Dylan, food and drink provided by all.

Later in the evening, after Saturday's Vigil Mass, Fr Denis Dennehy arrived and merged readily and very easily into the celebratory environment. At some stage during the evening, he placed a small package into my hand, the opening of which revealed an unusually shaped cross on a chain. He informed me it was the Cross of Brigid and that it was an ancient Irish custom to either wear or display this iconic cross to deter evil or disease. It was beautifully molded in pewter with an enhancing central piece of Connemara jade. Graciously, I offered my sincere thanks and during the ensuing week my journey towards Brigid became a reality.

Our parish community had been free of the paedophile priest for less than two years and although Irish-born Denis was doing all in his power to be a priest to the people, our parish community was in no way free of the paedophilic legacy. The unexpected receipt of such an unusual gift was impetus enough to want to know more about this mystical woman, her place in history and the significance of the cross itself. I was immediately deeply drawn to the symbolism, mystery, and promise of the ancient Brigid … Brigit, Brighid, Brihid, Brid, Bride, Bridie. Legend had honoured many Brigids throughout Ireland and some writers claim that Brigid was the goddess of the Sacred Flame of Kildare and the patron goddess of the Druids; that she was the goddess of upland areas, maintaining a wonderful hearth and portraying elevated characteristics such as wisdom, high intelligence, poetic eloquence, healing abilities, druidic knowledge, even blacksmithing skills. Clearly, the ancient, non-Christian Brigid and the early Christianised Brigid sustained a similar heart, one of boundless compassion and empathy.

Whether goddess or saint, regardless of what era or place she occupied, Brigid the woman is constantly presented as one who walked with justice and peace in her heart. Like her fellow Celts, she was consciously connected to the natural world, and was a woman of grace and independent spirit, of hospitality, compassion and dedication, of imagination, determination and inclusion, a seeker of justice.

Wherever the absolute truth of Brigid lies, I fell in love with the intrinsic nature of the ancient Brigid. I had discovered a woman who would forever impact my thinking about my place in the world. Aspects of her story and spirit seemed somehow familiar, entwined, sustaining, as I continued to search for ways to live with purpose during those dreadfully harrowing years of extremely frustrating and heartbreaking experiences with Church authorities, seeking justice for brutalised little boys. Her spirit carried me as my faith in the human spirit, and especially the Catholic Christian spirit, declined and then died an unendurable death.

I had not encountered the ancient Irish woman Brigid since my 1960's Wangaratta schooldays. Then, in 1984, she inadvertently re-entered my life and psyche just when I desperately needed a sign of hope: something to hold on to as I managed my journey with the unattended tragedy of sexual abuse of past students. The gift-giver was our Irish-born parish priest, Denis Dennehy, Mortlake's unwitting replacement for the predatory paedophile, Gerald Ridsdale. I wore that necklace constantly in all situations, by day and by night, until somehow, mysteriously and without any conscious provocation, it slipped from my neck, disappearing forever. It was most likely trampled underfoot as my husband and I negotiated our way from the airport train to the taxi rank of

Rome's Roma Termini Station. Of all cities! The year was 2004 and my original Brigid's Cross was unintentionally lost in the initial days of our 3 months of travel, within a hair's breadth of the home base of the Roman Catholic Church. Serendipitous?

It certainly was not difficult to warm to the essence of this woman, and I always remember the circumstances of my introduction to her with great fondness. My Brigid's Cross is permanently around my neck, nearing amulet status. I often find my fingers unconsciously at my throat; consciously connecting to her spirit. I have already gifted two granddaughters with a Brigid's Cross in acknowledgement of their having reached teenage years and the beginnings of womanhood whilst a third lies in wait for my third granddaughter until she too attains the same status. My dream is that they will choose to walk in Brigid's footsteps. Footsteps steeped in kindness and truth whilst they negotiate, and engage with, this increasingly complex, self-centered and destructive world into which they are emerging.

Consequently, when John suggested that my written story should not only be known to the Ballarat Catholic Diocesan community but should also be represented by an individual block on the '*Quilt of Hope*': a block displaying the Brigid's Cross, I could but respond in the affirmative, with passion. It represents my journey for truth, justice and hope.

Endnotes

[1] Jonas, A and Aroozoo, M. "Limitations of Actions (Child Abuse) Bill 2015". Parliament of Victoria, N.D. http://www.parliament.vic.gov.au

Chapter 8

Lives Lost

"The truth hurts but silence kills."
Mark Twain

The eight Red Doves on the Quilt of Hope represent the countless suicides and premature deaths linked to clerical child sexual abuse.

On the first day of the Royal Commission hearings in Ballarat in May 2015, a survivor held a photo of his Grade 4 St Alipius class from 1974. He stated:

> *Of the 33 boys in that image, I know that 12 are dead. I believe they committed suicide"*[1,2].

Further accounts followed throughout the hearings and multiple witnesses stated they knew of classmates both at St Alipius and St Patrick's College they believed had taken their lives due to being sexually abused as children. Another statement was as follows:

> *I believe the Church's handling of the abuse has, in some ways, been worse that the initial sexual abuse that occurred.*

The Story of the Quilt of Hope

The abuse might be historic, but the suicides by victims of child sexual abuse are still going, it is still happening.

Five men who were in my class at St Alipius have, in my view, committed suicide. I know an additional nine men who went to St Alipius whom I also believe have since committed suicide.

The suicides have left an impact on me too. I have been and continue to be impacted by the grief and loss of losing other victims of Brother Best to suicide, some of whom were my family, brothers and cousins.

I have had to bury people as a result of the trauma caused by these crimes. I have had to go to funerals where the person took their own life. I knew they were childhood sexual assault victims of Brother Best[3].

Had they lived, these boys would at the time have barely been fifty years old. The victims' shame and despair within a culture of secrecy and push-back from the Catholic hierarchy has ensured that we will never have access to all the stories behind these suicides. There can be little doubt, however, that most – perhaps all - were linked to clerical sexual abuse that we know was rampant at St. Alipius[4].

The Red Doves displayed on the Quilt also serve to honour the work undertaken by Detective Sergeant Kevin Carson. Within a culture of scepticism and denial, Kevin Carson fought for decades to bring criminal justice to prolific predators and shine light on the connection between clerical sexual child abuse and the high suicide toll in Ballarat. In his attempts to uncover further truths and seek a form of justice for those both passed and living, Kevin was internally and publicly discredited and maligned.

This chapter highlights a system unwilling to investigate and an institution unwilling to take responsibility. It tells part of the lived experience of Detective Sergeant Kevin Carson during a time when so much energy was being directed at active denial.

※※※

In April 2012, *The Age* published details of the confidential police reports Detective Sargent Kevin Carson had compiled. The reports suggested that between 2001 and 2011 in Victoria, 43 suicides were linked to clerical sexual abuse. As noted in the article:

> *Throughout the lengthy inquiries into clerical child sexual abuse perpetrators, investigators had discovered an inordinate number of suicides which appear to be a consequence of sexual offending...*
>
> *The number of people contacting this office to report members of their family, people they know, people they went to school with, who have taken their lives is constant. It would appear that an investigation would uncover many more deaths as a consequence of clergy sexual abuse*[5].

The community was shocked, but the Church denied knowledge of the abuse or its consequences. Four days later, the Victorian Parliamentary Inquiry into the Handling of Child Abuse by Religious and Other Non-Government Organisations was announced.

Row 6 Block 47
Drawn by Anne Lewis and embroidered by Beryl Andersen for Eilleen Piper, mother of Stephanie Piper.

The Story of the Quilt of Hope

Calls were made for the Victorian Coroner to reopen the cases in Kevin Carson's report. After considering the matter, the Coroner referred it back to Victoria police in July 2012 for further investigation. The police named their own investigation, 'Operation Plangere'. This was not publicly known, and only certain members of Victoria Police were privy to the investigation.

In November 2012, less than two weeks after the Victorian Parliamentary Inquiry had commenced, the confidential 'Operation Plangere' report was handed down. The report concluded that only 1 of the 43 nominated cases could be substantiated and reasoned that there was insufficient data to verify the other cases. The recommendation was that that no further action was required by Victoria Police.

In 2013 Detective Sergeant Kevin Carson made a personal submission to the Victorian Parliamentary Inquiry and then in 2014 provided evidence to the Royal Commission. At this time, he was not aware that the Operation Plangere investigation had occurred nor was he privy to the resulting Intelligence Brief. In good faith, he provided evidence that he was unaware of any investigations that had arisen from the reports he had written. The institution that he had dedicated years of service to had allowed this to occur, knowing the Plangere Report disputed his evidence.

The Plangere Report was not made publicly available until May 2015, when it was released as an exhibit by the Royal Commission. Within months *The Australian* published an 'exclusive' that 'exposed' the Victoria Police for "vastly overstating the number of suicides related to child-sex abuse by Catholic clergy"[6]. The article criticised Victoria Police for holding this information for over two years without correction and questioned evidence provided to the Victoria Parliamentary Inquiry by members of Victoria Police.

Row 5 Block 33
Unknown Maker

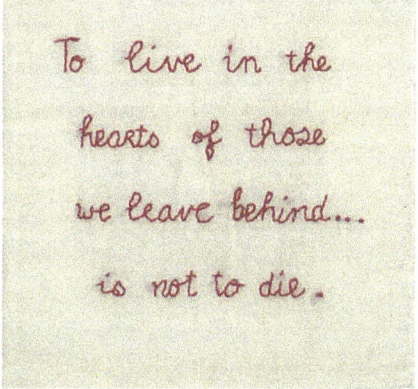

Row 5 Block 39
Made by Lyn Snibson

Defenders of the Church were outraged and continued the narrative that the Church was being unfairly vilified, and that the extent of clerical child sexual abuse was being overstated. The concern was for the damage caused to the Church's reputation rather than that of victims and their families. Kevin Carson's integrity was questioned and deficiencies in his reports were portrayed as incompetent police work.

For survivors, advocates, and those with the lived experience of knowing family members and friends who had taken their lives, the outcome of Operation Plangere was reprehensible. The investigation appeared cursory. For example, many of the

The Story of the Quilt of Hope

survivors and families of victims listed in the initial reports were not contacted by investigators to seek further information. This also included Kevin Carson, the author of the reports and who would have been well placed to provide additional information for the investigation. Judy Cortin, a long-time advocate and lawyer, commented at the time of the report being released:

> *This incompetently researched and at times inconsistent review assessed the prefatory reports of Detective Sergeant Kevin Carson, of Ballarat police, who had gathered data about the 43 men between 2001 and 2011 while investigating the sexual crimes of Ridsdale and Best.*
>
> *Carson had stated clearly that the information in his reports "would by no means be complete"; they were never intended to amount to a final and comprehensive report. He requested that the coroner reopen and further investigate these cases... These findings of Operation Plangere are flawed, worthless and misleading.*[7]

Row 1 Block 3
Unknown Maker

Row 10 Block 79
Unknown Maker

In her book 'Cardinal', Louise Milligan leave the reader in little doubt about the extensive failings of Operation Plangere. This included inexplicable failings to interview a range of individuals who were in a strong position to confirm Kevin Carson's findings[8]. Echoing the experiences of former Detective Dennis Ryan[9] in Mildura and former Detective Chief Inspector Peter Fox[10] in the Hunter Valley, Kevin was excluded from conducting any further investigations and threatened for speaking out against a system that has conspired to cover up the truth of clerical child sexual abuse.

In May 2015 Kevin Carson sought access to Operation Plangere as it appeared to contradict evidence he had provided to the Royal Commission. He was informed that it was a "protected document" and was not permitted to view the report. After multiple attempts to access the report, he concluded:

I can only assume from the refusal to allow me access to the daily log of Operation Plangere, that the contents of the log contains adverse reference to me in some capacity which could explain why I never knew an investigation was even taking place. Alternatively, I can only assume that Operation Plangere was conducted in 2012 to achieve a desired result[11].

In February 2016, Detective Sargent Kevin Carson provided a 219-page submission to the Royal Commission and then an addendum in April of the same year to provide further evidence he had gathered. This provided him with the opportunity to address commentary questioning the rigour of his work and his professional integrity.

What follows is an abridged version of his submission and addendum. It allows a portion of Kevin's lived experience of this time to be told with his words.

***

Taken from Royal Commission into Institutional Child Sexual Abuse submission, February 2016.

During the investigations of Ridsdale and Best over a number of years, information regularly came to my attention, primarily from

Ballarat East, and former students of St Alipius Primary School with regards to suicides and premature deaths that had occurred. To my surprise, information also came from other areas and other people that I had spoken to from various areas of the State.

I revisited all the documents which had been obtained during both investigations and spoke to people about the circumstances in which a number of the people had committed suicide or died prematurely. I felt the need to highlight these deaths and perhaps get something done about them. After reading the Coroner's Act, I thought that the Coroner might be interested in knowing about the number of deaths that appeared to be associated with clergy child sexual abuse.

…I have spoken to so many people who have indicated so much sadness, which is clearly a result of clergy sexual abuse. The Royal Commission has heard so much evidence of deaths and the link between suicides and premature deaths being associated with clergy child sexual abuse is now very clear.

…I refer to the premature deaths in Ballarat. Many survivors and families have tirelessly campaigned for the truth, for justice, to be believed and for their pain to be acknowledged. The long lasting and destructive effects of child sexual abuse are well documented in research and evidence before this Commission, the Victorian Parliamentary and other inquiries. These survivors, these victims, these families deal with the effects on a daily basis.

After 22 years of investigating these abuses, I recall the grieving mothers and families. I recall the 'children' that are not here to be able to tell their story of abuse and survival against adversity. I have a moral and sworn obligation to every person who trusted me with their story of horrific abuse.

Unfortunately, it is far too easy for people to sit in offices…and question my integrity alleging I had fabricated the numbers of suicides. From behind a computer, you don't see the mother's tears. You don't see the partners devastated, raising children as a single parent without their father. You don't see men crying because they can't hold their children, unable to hug them, unable to bathe their own children. You don't make it up!!!

…To suggest that the premature deaths which I initially sought to be referred to the Coroner for investigation were fabricated is extremely disappointing.

I believe the Catholic Church and other institutions owe an enormous debt to the survivors who have often, to their own detriment, become the voice for those unable to speak about their abuse.

These children had their lives destroyed by predators. They were robbed of a normal life, happiness and enjoyment many of us take for granted.

I believe that the community of Ballarat has been devastated by the abuse of Ridsdale, Best and others. There has been so much sadness there. Something needs to be put in place to assist the survivors and prevent any more lives being lost.

I believe families have been destroyed by devout parents unable to believe the horrific abuse against their children over their blind faith. A number of the victims I have spoken to during the course of my investigations have also told me of how the abuse has affected their family relationships. I recall interviewing a victim who had offended against the Christian brothers in anger, whilst his mother sat in the next room reciting the rosary. I believe families will continue to be destroyed until such time the hierarchy of the Church becomes accountable. Until the hierarchy of the Church challenges the victim blaming and starts talking to the families that have been destroyed and helping them understand, that yes, members of this Church betrayed their faith. Their children were abused.

For me, the impact on this community is found at our local cemeteries. Where children are buried, who died prematurely many having been raped, beaten and abused in a pervasive acceptance of this criminality which allowed the abuse to continue. For some, their parents are still living. I know there are still so many victims still unable to talk about what happened to them. How do we help them?

Taken from "Addendum to Statement dated 9th February 2016. Submitted 26th April 2016

I have been a member of the Victoria Police since 1974 and have seen some terrible things occur over that time. I have investigated the most serious of offences and have endeavoured to seek justice for victims in order to keep the community safe. Of all the investigations I have conducted, nothing comes close to what some members of the Catholic Church have done to children. Nothing comes close to the terrible way in which the church has covered things up. Nothing comes close to the damage and hurt caused to so many people.

Like any person who commits a serious offence, the community expects justice and in most circumstances punishment. The Catholic Church have proven that they have not been good citizens over a long period of time. They may have reformed somewhat but have not been punished for what they have done to children and what they have covered up.

As a Catholic, I am ashamed that the Royal Commission has had to endure so much horrific heart-breaking evidence from victims. To me the victims are the experts and should be believed.

✳✳✳

Detective Sergeant Kevin Carson is well known to survivors and the families of victims of clerical child sexual abuse. Without his unending support, many would never have taken criminal action against their perpetrators and criminal justice would not have been served. Prolific predators would not have been made accountable and light would not have been shone on the inertia of the Church in taking action against clerical child sexual abuse.

On Australia Day, 2021 Kevin received an Australian Police Medal in recognition of his years of service investigating child sexual abuse and providing support to victims and families. An acknowledgement that was overdue given what the preceding decades had presented to him.

Carmel Moloney met Kevin when she hand-delivered a copy of the Moving Towards Justice document printed in 2015. She first knew of Kevin in 2010 from Margot, her friend whose son Michael had provided a statement regarding his abuse by Brother Best (see Chapter 4). As Carmel followed the Best case, she knew of the support Kevin was providing to all the victims that were giving evidence in court. As the years progressed, she continued to hear words of gratitude, respect and admiration for Kevin from all those that had had dealings with him. His level of care shown to victims and their families is unsurpassed as is his dedication to bringing criminal justice to clerical sexual abuse offenders and their institution. It was without hesitation that we wanted to acknowledge Kevin in this chapter.

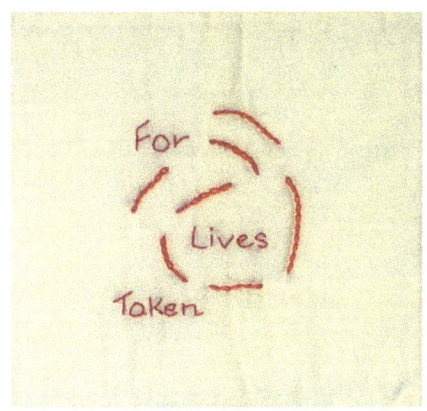

Row 6 Block 43
Unknown Maker

Row 7 Block 54
Unknown Maker

Endnotes

1. Royal Commission into institutional responses to child sexual abuse. (2015). Case study 28 transcript: Catholic Church authorities in Ballarat. Retrieved from http://www/childabuseroyalcommission.gov.au
2. When asked to consider these figures, a family policy analyst with expertise in demography and mental health made the following comment

    Starting with an approximate incidence of completed suicide in young males of 20 per 100,000 per annum, I multiplied by 40 (years) and it still comes in at under 1%. In practice, rates at school ages are lower. I checked back historically, and overall suicide rates were higher in the 1960s and 1970s than now but there have been intermediate times when rates were less than now. What it comes down to is that even a large adjustment for official rates being lower than "actual suicides" you wouldn't expect more than one case from a class of 33 boys. Most of the errors in arriving at this are conservative.

    These figures leave little doubt that something significant happened to many of these children in the Grade 4 class at St Alipius. In the context of what we know was happening in Ballarat at the time, the most likely explanation for the evidence presented to the Royal Commission would be these children's experience of sexual abuse.

3. https://www.childabuseroyalcommission.gov.au/sites/default/files/STAT.0584.
4. http://brokenrites.org.au/drupal/search/node/suicide
5. McKenzie, N, Baker, R and Lee, J. "Church's suicide victims". The Age. (13/4/2021). https://www.theage.com.au/national/victoria/churchs-suicide-victims-20120412-1wwox.html
6. Cops' false claim on abuse deaths. (2015, July 29). The Australian. Retrieved from http://www.theaustralian.com.au
7. Courtin, J. (2015, August 8) Flawed report denies justice to clergy-sex victims. The Sydney Morning Herald. Retrieved from http://www.smh.com.au
8. Milligan, L. (2019) *Cardinal: New Revelations: The rise and fall of George Pell.* Melbourne: Melbourne University Press. (See especially Chapters 10 and 17)
9. Ryan, D. & Hoysted, P. (2018). *Unholy Trinity* (2nd ed). Crows Nest: Allen & Unwin.
10. Fox, P. (2019). *Walking towards thunder.* Sydney: Hachette Australia.
11. Carson, K. (2016). Submission to Royal Commission into Institutional Responses to Child Sexual Abuse.

Chapter 9

Patchwork of Lives

"Awareness requires a response. From those that are aware much is expected. What is hidden cannot be healed."
Dr Jim Lawless

The Quilt of Hope weaves together the lived experiences of families whose children were abused and damaged by the Catholic church.

It was not possible to identify all the Quilt block makers or to record in-depth accounts of the lived experiences behind each of the blocks.

What follows are words given to us in letters from mothers and parishioners. They provide a glimpse of their experiences and offer further insight to the impact of clerical child sexual abuse.

***

Lindsay and Margaret

Lindsay and Margaret's son Geoff was sexually abused by Ridsdale when on a trip with the local gem club. Margaret embroidered a block containing the words "Our Son Geoff 1963 – 2011".

Lindsay and Margaret were married for over 66 years and both died in 2021.

The Moving Towards Justice members first learnt of their experiences when Lindsay approached them in Warrnambool when the Quilt was on display in the church foyer. He introduced himself simply by pointing to the block his wife Margaret had made and said, "That's my son".

Margaret writes about the abuse of their son Geoff:

Geoffrey was a shy little boy with 4 sisters - one younger and 3 older. His shyness was inherited from his grandparent (according to a child psychologist). This led to him not taking early schooling and he consequently had learning difficulties in reading.

We heard from the SPELD Society in Melbourne where we got help from an amazing teacher who chose me to be his teacher with visits and follow up advice in Melbourne every 6 weeks. Geoff responded and his education began.

He was always interested in nature, and I decided to join the local gem club where we met everyone monthly for meetings and workshops. Unfortunately for Geoff, Ridsdale was the President and through that contact got Geoff's respect. He offered him and two others a trip to a beach when they were to stay at the presbytery – he chose Geoff to share his room. Enough said!! Next day Geoff (too shy to know how to get in touch with us) hid in the reeds on the beach all day but had to go back for the night. The abuse continued!

Geoff never gave us any reasons to know what he had suffered and never confided in his sisters. The first we knew was just prior to his marriage – devastation for us then! He started drinking to forget and after 3 little daughters, his wife left him. From then on, his "drinking to forget" ruined his health and he was warned by his doctor that he was killing himself.

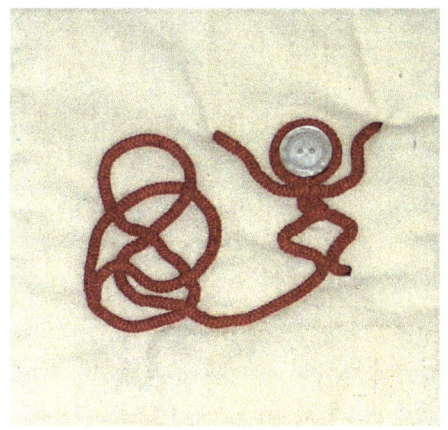

Row 2 Block 11
Made by Kathleen Moran
Our Lady untying the knots of the Church

Row 4 Block 26
Margaret, mother

We saw him twice on the Christmas Day but he was feeling too sick to come home to a family gathering. We took his present to him that evening and jellies that I'd been making for him each day as he couldn't keep any food down.

When we went on Boxing Day to see how he was feeling, we found him where he'd dropped on the floor dead.

***

'Mary'[1]

Mary created three blocks for the Quilt to honour her son and daughter along with a priest she admired. Her son and daughter were sexually abused by Ridsdale in the late 1970s when they were

12 and 11 years old. The abuse happened on the night of their father's funeral when after conducting the service, Ridsdale offered to take them for the night.

It would be over 20 years later when Mary became aware of the abuse due to court action against Ridsdale.

Mary writes:

May 19th 1975 was the very worst day of my life or so I thought. That was the day my husband was killed in an accident on our farm. He died in the arms of our middle daughter Tracey *while our eldest son went for help (no mobile phones then). She was 11 years old. She became very withdrawn and didn't really smile for a couple of years.*

Some 16 years later rumours started about Father Gerald Ridsdale who had been Parish Priest at Apollo Bay in the early 70's and celebrated Mass at Gellibrand where our family went to Mass on a regular basis.

One day my phone rang and Tracey *said "can I come home on Friday with* Fiona*" (strange silly question), "I have something to tell you".*

Nothing said until Sunday morning when I had to get milk and she came with me and asked to drive up to the gardens where she handed me a letter saying "I can't talk about it so I've written it all down".

That day I realised there are worse things in life than death.

What to do about it – where to start?

Then I discovered that our youngest son Shane *was also abused. Later still our eldest son* Tom *told me Gerald Ridsdale had tried it on him and he told to him to get lost!*

After my husband's funeral, Gerald Ridsdale asked me if he could take Shane *and* Tracey *back to Inglewood for the weekend where he had transferred from Apollo Bay and I let them go – the worst decision I ever made. It still haunts me to this day.*

Then the committal hearing and court case. My two children had decided not to appear but then they were both subpoenaed as their evidence was vital due to date, time etc that couldn't be disputed. Tracey was the first witness called and when she entered the court and saw Gerald Ridsdale she just froze and had to be escorted to the witness box by the detective. He was so kind and supportive through the whole ordeal. The questioning of both my children wasn't too bad but in regard to some of the other boys (young men) it was horrendous to the point of the Judge intervening.

Then the actual court case. Tracey was especially affected by some CWL ladies called as character witnesses for Gerald Ridsdale, but as I tried to explain to her, that was the man they knew. Even my own sister couldn't believe he was guilty as she knew him so well through the Gem Club. She wrote to him in prison for some time after he was convicted.

Over the years Shane had been a very angry young man who still says the ordeal didn't affect him. But a period of smoking dope and two failed marriages speaks for itself.

Tracey's first marriage was a disaster. The only good thing to come out of that a lovely granddaughter. Later she married again, but she just can't live in the married state – they are still friends.

The whole business has affected the family and extended family in various ways. A lot have left the church. My own faith was really challenged but then I decided that if I gave up my faith, he kept winning all along the way. As far as the Church is concerned, not a lot of help at the time. Father Shane McKinely and much later Father Michael O'Toole were good.

One evening my phone rang and a very drunk man spoke to me. I was at the point of hanging up when I realised it was Geoffrey and he said he rang up to apologise. "For what Geoffrey?" I ask and he said, "If I had spoken our earlier, your children would have been safe." As I said to him, he was just a child. How heart breaking. Not long after the conversation Geoffrey was dead.

In the beginning he (Ridsdale) talked of love and then the intimidation and fear set in. If you tell your mother, she won't believe you – she's a good Catholic – then later something bad will happen to her. Tracey had lost a father; she couldn't risk losing her mother.

***

Stephanie

Stephanie was active in church life and a member of the Catholic Women's League for twenty years. As was the case for many parishioners, she was unaware of the atrocities being committed within her church until revelations emerged.

Stephanie created a block featuring a heart motif with the phrase "the heart of friendship" and wanted to contribute some words to the book to share her voice.

Stephanie recalls her experiences:

Quite some years ago now, when Child Abuse by clerics was not known about as it is today, I attended a Conference at Terang in Western Victoria. At the time the Chaplain for the organisation was Father Gerald Ridsdale. He had been present at the Conference and when we were tidying up someone called out that he had left his case behind and did anyone go home through Mortlake where Fr Ridsdale was Parish Priest. As it happened, I went that way so offered to return the case to him.

When I got to the presbytery, I was surprised to find three little boys – probably about or 8 all busy in the garden. One had a little wheelbarrow, another was pulling weeds, and the third carrying things in and out of the shed. I immediately thought how nice it was that Fr Ridsdale got on so well with these children, and good also, that the children seemed to be quite happy being there! Such was my ignorance about the way paedophiles worked. At that time, I knew very little about these things because to my knowledge, things like this had not occurred anywhere close to where I lived.

In my innocence I just went on as before, until a few weeks later there was a Diocesan gathering in Warrnambool which I attended. While there, I joined a conversation of a number of people, a lot of whom were teachers in the Catholic schools. One in particular was a teacher at Mortlake. To my horror the conversation was about some of the scandals that had been happening, including at Mortlake. The teacher's problem was what to do about it. Apparently, they had tried to contact the Bishop but got no satisfaction.

It was only a few short weeks afterwards, that the whole thing exploded and we all now know what the outcome was.

I have never forgotten those little boys and because I had no idea who they were I have no idea what might have happened to them. Please God, they did not suffer from their experience.

✱✱✱

Row 9 Block 71
Made by Stephanie Kent

Row 3 Block 22
Maker Unknown

Gwen

Gwen first met Carmel and Lyn (Moving Towards Justice members) through Sr Pam Barlow who had facilitated the display of the Quilt of Hope in a gallery in Edenhope. Pam suggested they meet with Gwen and her husband as she knew their story and the isolation they had suffered.

Gwen became aware of clerical child sexual abuse through her nursing and community services work. There were whispers in the community of inappropriate behaviour but no-one around her seemed to want to act.

She recalled to Carmel the moment when she approached the local priest to express concern about clerical child sexual abuse. The response she received was stony silence and after some time had passed, she felt stupid and left.

The words contributed by Gwen provide the opportunity for her voice to be heard. As many others experienced, she was shunned by her community for speaking out against the Church and horrified others were more interested in protecting the church than those who were suffering.

Gwen writes of her experiences as a parishioner:

About 45 years ago a friend and her husband invited my family to dinner.

She settled the men and children by the fire and took me to another room. She was uneasy about our new priest as it had been suggested to her that he had been sent to our parish from a parish where he had been abusing altar boys.

We both had a poor understanding of what that actually involved.

As we both had very young children in our care, neither of us quite knew what to think about this and selfishly didn't ever discuss this subject again.

I live to regret that decision. If only I had made it my business to try to understand.

Twenty-five years later I had my first meeting with a victim - a shattered, devastated young man who still to that day was struggling to understand the meaning and the reason for his abuse by the parish priest who was so respected by his family and fellow parishioners. He constantly wondered what he must have done to cause this.

John told me he was 12 years old when the abuse started. He thought sometimes that maybe it was the Church trying to teach him about his sexuality. John told me 'Rids was at our home for a meal in the evening so often that I thought maybe my mother was aware of what was happening'.

John felt isolated from his school and parish community and became very lonely in his thoughts.

One day John told me he drove to Ballarat and travelled by train to Melbourne, having made an appointment to see the Archbishop. He anticipated being able to finally tell his story to someone in authority in the Church.

John had a major infection in his leg as the result of a car accident. He was far from well. He told me he limped up to the Cathedral at East Melbourne. He said he did not get a chance to tell his story. Rather, he recalled the Archbishop pushing some cash across his desk while asking something like, "Will this do?"

John said he fled in tears. He did not touch the money. Instead he limped back to the station arriving home late that night.

When I saw John next, he was a broken devastated young man.

I think it was about this time the abuse became general knowledge in the parish and wider community of our small town. It was never openly talked about although I did hear some hushed talk about the parish priest.

The Story of the Quilt of Hope

The community did not cope with the upheaval within the parish and never openly discussed it and so it festered along for years. It seemed to me that they wanted to get on with being 'good Catholics' and it would all blow over.

I found their attitude to John and other victims as troublemakers as most disturbing.

The story of our parish angered my husband and me and we held resentment that no one else seemed to be angry. It shattered and puzzled us to the point where we have isolated ourselves from the Catholic church.

At the time the offending took place and in the following years it seemed we as Catholics had a tendency to be almost self-righteous about the process of being 'good Catholics' rather than practising our Christian faith in a loving, caring and forgiving God.

The power and attitude of the church has been dehumanising of us, the parishioners.

Row 8 Block 61
Shirley Edgar, parishioner

"As fishermen live in hope of a catch, I have used this image as a sign of my hope that those I know who have been abused and have not come forward may one day find peace and sense of calm in their lives. One of these men in particular is now suffering doubly because he now sees himself as weak for not coming forward. These men all love the outdoor life so fishing seems a pertinent image of them."

The Sisters of Mercy

The Sisters of Mercy provided ongoing support to Moving Towards Justice and the Quilt of Hope throughout the decades of action.

This included active participation as members of MTJ and providing meeting space in the early stages of the Quilt development.

In the course of the Royal Commission hearings in Ballarat, they provided a quiet space for the Quilt to be displayed and created a prayer card featuring the Quilt. The card invited people to collectively, "pray for healing for all persons who have been hurt by abuse".

The Sisters of Mercy contributed 10 embroidered blocks to the Quilt.

A special acknowledgement is given to Sr Rita Hayes, Sr Anne Forbes, Sr Kathleen Moran and Sr Pam Barlow in appreciation of their generosity in opening their hearts and home to a small group of Catholic laity.

Row 1 Block 2

Row 8 Block 64

The Story of the Quilt of Hope

Row 9 Block 66

Row 2 Block 15

Row 7 Block 52

Row 10 Block 77

Row 5 Block 35

Row 4 Block 25

Row 6 Block 46 *Row 3 Block 21*

Endnotes

1 To preserve anonymity, all names in this story have been changed.

RECOMMENDED READING

Feenan, P. (2012). *Holy hell.* Fremantle: Fontaine Press.

Foster, C and Kennedy, P. (2011). *Hell on the way to heaven.* Sydney: Random House.

Fox, P. (2019). *Walking Towards Thunder: The true story of a whistleblowing cop who took on corruption and the Church.* Sydney: Hachette Australia.

Gero, A. (2008). *The Fabric of Society: Australia's quilt heritage from convict times to 1960.* Australia: The Beagle Press.

Hunter, C. (2019). *Threads of Life: A history of the world through the eye of a needle.* Great Britain: Sceptre.

Milligan, L. (2019). *Cardinal: New Revelations: The rise and fall of George Pell.* Carlton: Melbourne University Press.

Morris-Marr, L. (2019). *Fallen: The inside story of the secret trial and conviction of Cardinal George Pell.* Crows Nest: Allen and Unwin.

Ryan, D and Hoysted, P. (2018). *Unholy Trinity.* Crows Nest: Allen & Unwin.

Smith, S. (2020). *The Altar Boys.* Sydney: Harper Collins.

POSTSCRIPT

"The ones who have a voice must speak for those who are voiceless."
Archbishop Oscar Romero

The Quilt of Hope is a powerful memorial that pays homage to the multitude of lives that have been impacted by clerical child sexual abuse. It also represents the actions of a few that when faced with unbearable truths courageously chose to act and be a voice for change.

This book has been written to honour the Quilt and the voices behind the blocks. The lived experiences of mothers, parishioners and truth seekers presented in the book are sadly not unique and are synonymous with what others have endured.

We see this book as another step forward in breaking the silence and offering hope to those that have still not been heard or believed. There are stories yet to be told as the makers behind the blocks continue to be identified and provided with the opportunity to speak their truth.

May we all be willing to make a stand in the face of evil and know that our actions can make a difference in people's lives.

APPENDIX A

Ann Ryan's Letter to the Priest

Dear ………………....,

Re: Silence in the Church on matters of sexual abuse by clergy

I write out of friendship and concern, and in solidarity … so please give my thoughts the respect and time I believe is warranted.

    I really don't know where to begin other than to say that, as a Church member, I am really hurting, and I have been for some years, at the Church's stance, i.e., its public stance regarding sexual abuse within it. Why has the Church taken action on behalf of the offender while the pain of the victim has gone unaddressed? Why has it chosen not to acknowledge the hurt, and continued suffering of victims, caused by the behaviour of some clergy? Why, when we are asked to be people of forgiveness, can't the Church ask forgiveness of its members? Does the institutional Church consider itself above human failing? After all, it is a human body according to Paul. What has become of the Church's credibility? What will continue to happen to it if methods that work against humanity are continually used? Why are the structures silent? Why are the priests silent? Do they understand the extent of the hurt of the victims and their families? Do they know of the many lives that have been permanently damaged? How much truth are they in touch with? Do they have any idea of the number of victims throughout the diocese? [Mortlake has 8-10 at least]. And yet that one priest lived in at least ten parishes! Think about the human cost … can it really go unchallenged? How can we truly live with ourselves as Church, in such a thundering silence of injustice and ugliness? What have YOU done to break this silence? What do YOU plan to do to break this silence?

My Story and where I'm coming from

Fortunately, my family is not directly affected, but in an indirect way we are, as are all families in the Mortlake parish. I was a teacher at St Colman's School during the early 80s when the offences were taking place. In fact, I taught the victims on a regular part-time basis. My daughter, Kate, was a friend and classmate of the victims! No-one had any idea as to what was going on … the boys were allowed to visit the presbytery at lunchtime, as the priest had Atari games and a pool table! We now know that was a ploy used to entice victims! Can you imagine the hurt and pain of the school principal? She was the person who gave permission and sent the boys, unwittingly, into the trap! Completely trusting! The parish was stunned and horrified when the truth eventuated … the priest had been moved on and no effort made by the Church to redress the issue, then or since … Life was to proceed as if nothing had taken place … the pretend game.

Like other parishioners I moved as if in a daze, looked at my boy pupils in a different light wondering who had been hurt, and how the affected families were coping with it all. And just how many had been hurt? The news provided answers for me regarding some of their behavioural patterns. It was so sad, and I felt so helpless! All doors were closed … until 1989 during 'Renew'. [The spirit moves in strange ways as I have discovered on more than one occasion.] I was working in Outreach and one day, without warning, a mother shared her deep anguish and sorrow with me. Her son had been offended against and was finding life very difficult e.g., he wouldn't trust adult men or be alone with them … he wouldn't visit a doctor alone … his relationship with his father was damaged … he found it difficult to apply himself to a job ... he found it difficult to trust and establish friendships. All these symptoms were directly attributable to the sexual abuse he had suffered, according to the counsellor at the sexual assault unit. The mother's pain was compounded by the fact that she insisted her son went to the altar boys' nights and, when he objected, she delivered him! She has had nowhere to take her pain, and have it healed nor have the other victims or their families. You might say that there are other counselling agencies, but these people were afraid of the disbelief, the publicity and the subsequent damage to the Church! Imagine That!

This particular mother was also instructed in the faith and confirmed by this priest ... she now feels dirty and degraded. Her mother, the victim's grandmother, was unaware until recently of the offences, so everything was done to prevent the grandmother from finding out ... she is still unaware that her grandson was offended against. This is only one boy and his family. Multiply that by 6-10 [a conservative number] and you have direct victims in Mortlake. Now multiply that by 9 [other parishes the priest lived in] and the picture <u>begins</u> to fall into focus! Since that initial sharing I have, through the help of this mother, been able to talk to two other families of victims ... parents only. [In fact, I have had contact today and further implications for concern have arisen. I shall mention these later.] These parents are in continual pain for many reasons: because of the permanent damage inflicted on their sons, because of their own guilt at not being aware of what was happening and because of the attitude of the institutional Church that said, through its attitude and inaction ... You and your pain are unimportant.

Because of the anguish of this mother, I decided to take action, so I wrote to the Bishop. We actually corresponded for a period of five months from late 1989 to early 1990. All the mother wanted was acknowledgement of the offences having taken place and an assurance that the priest would not be put in a position where he could re-offend ... causing pain she already knew. However, the Bishop failed to be moved to any sort of action other than to point to Diocesan Family Services! [A service associated with the very church which was refusing to acknowledge her pain!] This immobility was seen as rejection and disregard for the victims' pain and distress. In 1990, when the Bishop was in the parish for Confirmation, I approached him personally, in the privacy of the presbytery, to ask him to see one or more of the effected parents. He refused ... alleging legal implications!

<u>What would Jesus have done?</u> The question can be validly asked of you and me.

Since that time, I've felt trapped and unable to be pro-active other than to listen to parents when sharing. Every conversation leads to the same place and no further. Now, I am a member of the Interim Diocesan Pastoral Council [I.D.P.C.] and, until recently, was questioning my connections with the institutional Church because I felt it was far too removed from the ordinary, struggling human being. I still feel this very deeply ... however, because of recent events ... namely the exposing of the truth regarding the priest in question ... I have found renewed strength, purpose and vision, and I intend to pursue justice and reconciliation with added gusto because I know, in my gut, that I am right, and that Jesus is behind it all!

As a consequence of this newfound energy, I raised and talked to the issue of the Silence of the Church at the last I.D.P.C. meeting on 24/09/93. I recounted my story and spoke about my concerns for the non-offending priests and their hurt being attended to... about the fact that my vision is for recognition of sexual abuse by clergy, and that reconciliation and healing be facilitated <u>within Church structures</u>. All of us being mended together ... <u>a collective strategy</u>. It could be such an experience of Church! The issue was well received, and it was obvious that all at the table were affected to some degree by the hurt and were anxious that the silence be broken.

From this meeting a letter was to be written to Fr John McKinnon in his capacity as Director of the Ministry to Priests, and hopefully would play some part in your meeting on 17/18 October.

Just now, unplanned, I rang the parents of the third family I've been able to share with and, on speaking to the mother, have come up against some further factual material re the priest in Mortlake which I was unaware of. He had only been in the parish two days when their fourteen-year-old son came home in an obvious state of shock saying, 'I think Father … might be gay', and recounted what had taken place. Both parents communicated with Ballarat the next day. As the Bishop was away, they spoke to the Vicar General, who met their concerns with disbelief and suggested that their child must have imagined it. On the evening of that same day the priest in question came to the family kitchen and reassured the family that nothing untoward had taken place. Almost two years later they discovered that their other two sons had been sexually abused by the same priest and they, along with another couple who also had two sons abused, one badly, went to speak with the Bishop.

According to her they were made to look like the criminal and the Bishop remained unmoved until she threatened police action. The priest was gone within days! [Chris Wilding of Broken Rites maintains this same priest was removed from Inglewood after only eight months because of threatened police action after allegations of sexual abuse!] This mother's testimony made me want to cry … she had not shared at such a level before, which is another sign of the spirit … her attitude has evolved into one of angry acceptance … 'you battle on, what else can you do?' One can understand her attitude after coping with three sexually abused sons and two unsatisfactory contacts with Ballarat looking for help. She says her boys' spirituality is ruined forever and that one now totally denies the events [his way of coping] and the youngest is fearful of his girlfriend finding out! When I invited her to write she was reticent as her anger is still very much alive and her feelings for other priests is one of concern. 'I feel desperately sorry for other priests.' She feels very strongly that there was, and still is, 'a strong conspiracy of silence and protection of the offender and what can you do about it?' Her feelings are supported by the fact that she and her husband contacted Ballarat at the beginning of the priest's term and two years later this same couple, along with another, saw the bishop, yet as I was led to believe from the bishop's letter of December 1989, 'there was no mention of any specific person or family or any specific action'.

After the priest left the parish at least one father of a victim went to Ballarat to see the Bishop. As the Bishop was overseas at the time, he was assured by the Vicar General that the matter would be attended to. He returned hopeful, but this hopefulness soon turned to disillusionment as time progressed and no action was initiated. I'm still wondering what the rest of the story is! It all contributes to the conspiracy of silence, and that they, as people and their inherent pain did not, and do not, count.

However, being an eternal optimist, I believe we can do much to initiate and facilitate the healing process. It will require special stamina and an ability to move beyond our own pain to the victims' pain. Only then will true and just reconciliation and healing take place. A public acknowledgment and apology would be a great beginning ... we will just have to endure any flak ... can it be any worse than it is now with this cancerous disease moving amongst us dragging down morale and sending people away from the Church? Maybe this era marks the end of the institutional Church as we've known it ... making way for something more relevant and credible! Deep down I believe this theory. However, the priests of the new model will not want to be trapped in the time warp of the conspiracy of silence. You need to throw off this illness to become well again. I believe the time is ripe, if not over-ripe!

My vision for healing within the Church

- Firstly, I would like to see the priests of the Ballarat diocese initiate and address action to facilitate their own healing.

- That they challenge the silence of the Church so that past mistakes are acknowledged.

- That reconciliatory processes are developed and put into action throughout the diocese.

- I would like to see the whole diocesan Church empowered to take part in the healing process.

- That procedures are put in place to disallow such evil taking place in the future.

- I would like to feel that truth and openness be sought at all times.

- That the whole process take place within a short time frame.

- That part of the reconciliation process be incorporated into next year's Diocesan Assembly.

Only then can the Church claim to be the living body of Christ, a place of justice, a place of forgiveness, nurture and healing'.

I have written to each of you as I know you in varying degrees and because I believe you need to be collectively proactive to restore vision and purpose to your roles, to restore belief in yourselves. Perhaps I also believe that some will have the courage to walk on water. You are needed to lead relevantly and with credibility ... the alternative is to suffer continued scorn and mistrust; the legacy of the silence and the hypocrisy. You cannot ask people to seek forgiveness in their lives if you are unable to do the same in yours! The world no longer accepts double standards from institutions which supposedly exist to serve the common person.

There is no doubt it will be difficult to be challenging and proactive, but I've had to overcome apprehension and doubt to write this letter to a group of priests working within a patriarchal institution! I was fearful, but now that I have acted, I'll be able to live with myself because I feel free ... knowing that it had to be done for the sake of the victims, and for the sake of truth, love and justice i.e. Jesus, who did more than empathise with human pain. On behalf of the victimised, he named and proclaimed the structures of oppression and he acted in solidarity with his disciples to liberate victims through symbolic acts of conscientious objection. He was not intimidated by men's laws!

In closing, I would like to draw attention to the March edition of 'Our Diocesan Community' which ran an article 'of vital concern'. It states that "the church loses credibility when these cases come to light, and even more so when no appropriate action is taken in good time, or even worse, by trying to cover up scandal". The Church needs to be loyal to its members ... as the institutional Church is, or should be, the servant of the people rather than the reverse situation.

Yours in the quest for love, truth and justice.

Ann Ryan

October 1993.

APPENDIX B

Noteable Australian Quilts

The Rajah Quilt (1841)

The Rajah Quilt was made by 180 female prisoners on board the Rajah travelling from England to Van Diemen's Land in 1841. Carrying needlecraft provisions for the four-month voyage, the materials were transformed into an embroidered and appliqued coverlet made up of inscribed patchwork that would become known as the Rajah Quilt.

Rediscovered in 1987 in an attic in Scotland, it was returned to Australia in 1989 and is held by the National Gallery of Australia who described it as:

> *a work of great documentary importance to Australia's history, it is also an extraordinary work of art; a product of beauty from the hands of many women who, while in the most abject circumstances, were able to work together to produce something of hope. Its story is one of hope and persistence and has been a central subject to study into colonial life since its rediscovery in 1987.*[1]

The Red and White Signature Quilts (WW1 & WW2)

The red and white signature quilts were popular during both the world wars and associated with the Red Cross[2]. One of note is the Gallipoli WW1 Red and White Embroidered Quilt made by Mrs Hansen and her friends during WWI. Mrs Hansen's son, Captain Stewart Murray Hansen, fought during WW1 with the 14th Battalion in Gallipoli, Turkey, and in France. Held at the Williamstown Historical Society, Victoria, the custodians depict the story behind the quilt as follows:

Mrs Hansen was a member of the Williamstown Anzac Club which sent comfort parcels direct to local soldiers at the front. These were wrapped in a calico bag which the soldier could use as a laundry bag, or to hold personal effects. Mrs Hansen and friends decided to use uniform square offcuts of calico as a fund raiser, by asking locals to sign their name on a space on a square and pay sixpence. As each square was filled, the ladies would stitch the signature in red cotton thread and bind the edges in red before assembling them as a quilt.

But the ladies decided to make their quilt "different" and so, Mrs Hansen sent squares to her son Stewart for him to collect the signatures of serving men he met, to post home for inclusion.

Stewart collected signatures of men from his 14th Battalion plus nurses, medics, doctors, members of the new Air Corps, Officers and even cooks and stewards. The squares, signed with pencil, were sent back to Australia, where they were embroidered in red silk by his mother and her friends, bordered by narrow strips of red material, and pieced together. After being wounded in France, Stewart continued to collect and did so up until he was mortally wounded in 1917.

His mother and friends continued to embroider and assemble the 72 squares, containing hundreds of Stewart's collected signatures, often with service numbers, rank, battalion included. The quilt is a permanent record of many men and women who served in WW1, many of whom never returned.[3]

The Changi Quilts: (1942-1944)

The Changi Quilts are the most famous WWII quilts. During 1942, three quilts were made for the British, Australian and Japanese Red Cross organisations by the women and nurses interned in Changi Prison (Singapore). Each quilt comprises 66 individual embroidered squares made from scraps of material and sewn together to form a patchwork quilt. Under the guise of making them for the wounded in Changi hospitals, the making of the quilts was intended to not only pass time but also to include hidden messages to the outside world or insert words of patriotism.[4]

The idea to make the quilts came from Mrs Ethel Mulvany, a Canadian Red Cross representative. She was inspired by a group of Girl Guides (aged 8 to 16 years) who created the Changi Girl Guide quilt as a surprise birthday present for their Guide leader, Elizabeth Ennis. Using a Grandmother's Flower Garden pattern, the girls collected scraps of material and met secretly to sew them together and embroider their names at the centre of each flower.

The Changi Quilts have come to be a symbol of those caught up in a war without a choice and a testament to the resilience of the women living through this experience.[5]

Both the Australian and Japanese Changi quilts are held at the Australian War Memorial in Canberra. The British Changi quilt can be viewed at the British Red Cross UK office in London.

Endnotes

1   The Rajah Quilt, (n.d.), National Gallery of Australia. https://nga.gov.au/rajahquilt/
2   Gero 2015 – is this a book or a website?
3   Marcus, A. "Sons of Williamstown". Williamstown Historical Society, 18/1/2019. https://www.williamstownhistsoc.org.au/author/mcasand/
4   The Australian War Memorial. "History of the Changi Quilts". Australian War Memorial. Updated 23/12/2019. https://www.awm.gov.au/articles/encyclopedia/quilt
5   *Threads of Life*, (p53), by Hunter, C, (2019), Australia: Harry N Abrams

www.ingramcontent.com/pod-product-compliance
Lightning Source LLC
Chambersburg PA
CBHW040740020526
44107CB00084B/2828